Bonhoeffer

A Screenplay

William Wilson

Johnston, Iowa

Dedicated to the memory of
Dietrich Bonhoeffer

Contents

BONHOEFFER

EXT. WOLF'S LAIR - DAY

Forested area. Nazi compound encircled by tall metal
fencing topped with barbed wire. German military
limousine pulls up. Colonel von STAUFFENBERG exits
with briefcase. He is in his 30s, tall, handsome, has
a patch over one eye, and is missing right hand.

Chauffeur leaves to park auto. Stauffenberg glances
around, squats, opens briefcase, lifts papers, flips back
cloth, uses tweezers to crush vial of acid inside bomb,
flings tweezers into underbrush, resets items, closes
briefcase, and trots up to first checkpoint. It is manned
by BRUNO, a not too bright, muscular SS Guard.
Stauffenberg shows ID, but holds onto briefcase.

                    STAUFFENBERG
          I'm late, Bruno. Make it quick.

                    BRUNO
          I check everything. Leave early next time.

                    STAUFFENBERG
               (handing him briefcase)
          My report today is not good. More replacements
          needed at the front. Shall I tell Hitler that
          you volunteer?

Bruno stops short of opening case and hands it back to
Stauffenberg.

                    BRUNO
          Funny man. Leave early next time.

Bruno opens gate. Stauffenberg hurries down path to second
checkpoint, which grants entry to Main Building. SCHMITZ
guards gate.

                    STAUFFENBERG
          Running late, Schmitz. Let me through.

                    SCHMITZ
          Have to check ID.

Stauffenberg hands him ID.

                    SCHMITZ
          Need to check the briefcase ... regulations.

                    STAUFFENBERG
                (handing him briefcase)
          You're going to make me late, Schmitz.

Schmitz opens briefcase. Papers on top. General BRANDT,
60s, pokes his head out of door.

                    BRANDT
          Stauffenberg. There you are. You're next.
          Forget it, Schmitz.

Schmitz looks at Brandt, then at Stauffenberg.
Stauffenberg eyes Schmitz, who slowly closes briefcase,
hands it to Stauffenberg, and opens gate. Stauffenberg
hustles to door and says to Brandt...

                    STAUFFENBERG
          Unbelievable headwind.

Brandt slaps Stauffenberg on back. Startled, Stauffenberg
steadies briefcase.

                    BRANDT
          Hey, kid. I said you would succeed, didn't I?
          This is the big time!

                    STAUFFENBERG
          Yes sir. I hope you are right.

Brandt puzzled. Stauffenberg notices. Their eyes lock
momentarily.

INT. HALLWAY - DAY

Stauffenberg and Brandt walk past desk manned by another
Guard. Stauffenberg speaks to Guard.

                    STAUFFENBERG
          I'm expecting an urgent call from Berlin. Let me
          know when it comes.

Begin GRADUALLY INCREASING RUSHING SOUND. Brandt opens
door and walks in. Stauffenberg stops, takes deep breath,
and follows.

INT. WAR ROOM - DAY

Sawhorses at either end support heavy oaken planks, forming
an 18' x 5' table covered with maps. HITLER is seated in
middle on long side, with back to door. Directly across
table, a General is reporting (silent to us). Brandt takes
seat. Fifteen others sit around table.

Hitler acknowledges Stauffenberg. General uses pointer to
emphasize location on map. Hitler turns attention to map,
takes magnifying glass, rises and leans over table to
inspect location being discussed. Several others do so as
well.

Stauffenberg approaches table, feigns interest in map, then
carefully places briefcase under table and pushes it toward
Hitler with foot. He then backs unnoticed towards door.
Brandt changes position for closer look and hits foot on
Stauffenberg's briefcase. Stauffenberg freezes. Hitler
looks back at Brandt, who looks under table, picks up
briefcase, sets it under far end of table, and returns to
map. RUSHING SOUND at its LOUDEST.

INT. HALLWAY - DAY

Stauffenberg rushes past Guard at desk. RUSHING SOUND
begins RECEDING GRADUALLY. Stauffenberg barely audible.

                    STAUFFENBERG
          Forgot something in the auto. Hold my call.

Guard rises ... but Stauffenberg is gone.

EXT. WOLF'S LAIR - DAY

Stauffenberg hurries to first gate.

                    STAUFFENBERG
          Forgot something in the auto.

Puzzled Schmitz opens gate. Stauffenberg hustles through.
He eyes Schmitz, then glances at building.

INT. WAR ROOM - DAY

Hitler turns to look for Stauffenberg, then looks at
Brandt, who looks toward briefcase, then locks eyes with
Hitler.

LOUD SPLASH!

EXT. BEACH - DAY

SIX-YEAR-OLD DIETRICH swims underwater. Our vision is
blurred as through his eyes we view siblings swimming
underwater as well. "BONHOEFFER" fades in/out screen
center, followed by "GERMANY", then "1912". We break water
and through Dietrich's nearsighted eyes notice something
flitting about on water's surface. We run toward
DIETRICH'S YOUNG MOTHER, sitting on blanket in sand on
crowded beach. Dietrich's sister SUSANNE, 3, is pointing
to siblings in the water.

                    SUSANNE
          Kawl-Fweedwick, Sabeeney, Kwistiney...

She points to Dietrich, then to herself as Dietrich's Young
Mother hands Dietrich his glasses.

                    SUSANNE
          ... Deetwick, Susanne!

After putting on small, wire-rimmed glasses (onto camera,
now in focus), Dietrich and we discover the flitting
something to be a dragonfly. We quickly shift to brief
close-up of dragonfly's eyes, then back to previous
perspective. We slowly pull away from Dietrich's head to
see a wet-haired, blonde-banged, young boy standing next to
Mother and focused intently on the dragonfly. LAUGHTER and
SPLASHING in the background.

                    SIX-YEAR-OLD DIETRICH
                    (to Mother)
          There is a creature over the water! Don't be
          afraid, I will protect you!

Mother smiles and hugs Dietrich, then catches twinkling
eyes of smiling YOUNG BEARDED MAN in swimsuit, sitting on
blanket behind and to their left. Back to close-up of
dragonfly's eyes, then to close-up of Dietrich's face.

LOUD MARCHING OF SOLDIERS.

INT. CLASSROOM - DAY

Face of FOURTEEN-YEAR-OLD DIETRICH, adjusting wire-rimmed
glasses. We pull away to reveal class of high school boys
seated in rows, each in high button-down collar and tie.
MASTER, similarly dressed, stands at front, pointer in
hand. Map of Europe hangs behind. "1920" fades in/out
screen center.

                    MASTER
          Treaty of Versailles. Evaluate.
               (pause)
          Mr. Wessler!

WESSLER snaps to stand next to desk.

                    WESSLER
          It is an abomination! It demands 132 billion
          marks in reparations, yet offers no help for
          rebuilding the infrastructure necessary to
          generate such funds. However, if the National
          Socialists were in power...

                    MASTER
               (cuts him off)
          Thank you, Mr. Wessler ... you may sit down.
               (pause)
          Versailles. Evaluate! Mr. Rosen!

ROSEN rises and stands next to desk.

                    ROSEN
          An abomination to be sure!
               (to Wessler)
          But the Nazis are not the answer, rather
          Communism, like that which has flowered in the
          Soviet...

                    MASTER
               (cuts him off)
          Thank you, Mr. Rosen ... YOU may sit down.

Wessler and Rosen fume at each other. Dietrich watches
anxiously.

                    MASTER
          Extremism, gentlemen ... whether from the Right
          or the Left? Is THAT the answer?
                    (sighs)
          Saner minds. How do you, Germany's brightest,
          plan to aid your nation?
                    (pause)
          Mr. Delbruck!

Startled DELBRUCK jumps up.

                    DELBRUCK
          Sir. I hope to study government and aid the
          Weimar in creating a just and lasting democracy.

                    WESSLER
          National Socialism!

                    ROSEN
                    (springing from seat)
          Communism!

Wessler jumps up and heads for Rosen.

                    MASTER
          Enough! ENOUGH! Sit down! NOW!

They return to seats and glare at each other. Dietrich
watches intensely. Master gathers himself.

                    MASTER
          THAT, gentlemen, is where extremism leads!
                    (calmly to Dietrich)
          And how does the son of the renowned
          psychiatrist, Dr. Karl Bonhoeffer, plan to aid
          his nation?

Dietrich responds clearly, calmly, but forgets to rise.

                    FOURTEEN-YEAR OLD DIETRICH
          I want to study theology.

Muffled gasps, snickers, stares, and frowns.

                    MASTER
          Then you have some surprises ahead of you.

Dietrich is puzzled by Master's comment.

LOUD MARCHING OF SOLDIERS.

INT. BONHOEFFER PARLOR - DUSK

Parlor full of well-dressed guests, some standing, some
seated. Children scurry about. Waiters serve from hand-
held trays. LAUGHTER, CONVERSATION. Four-String Quartet
provides BACKGROUND MUSIC. "1929" fades in/out screen
center.

Face of DIETRICH, mid 20s. We pull back to view him
standing in conversation with KARL-FRIEDRICH, 30s, HANS and
GERHARD, mid 20s.

                    HANS
          So, another Doctor Bonhoeffer.

                    KARL-FRIEDRICH
          Yes, but in theology.

Dietrich takes ribbing kindly.

                    HANS
          Hardly a solid subject, like science. Eh, Karl-
          Friedrich?

                    KARL-FRIEDRICH
          At least I can SEE my subject.

Light LAUGHTER.

EXT. BONHOEFFER HOME - DUSK

FRANZ, early 20s, hurries down sidewalk, turns up main
entrance, and past address plaque on brick pillar that
reads, "Marienburger-Allee 43". Servant opens door.

INT. BONHOEFFER PARLOR - DUSK

Franz enters, surveys scene, eyes Dietrich, and approaches
circle. Karl-Friedrich persists...

                    KARL-FRIEDRICH

What of it, Dietrich? Does God become more REAL
when one becomes lecturer in theology at the
university?

                    DIETRICH
He remains JUST as real.

                    KARL-FRIEDRICH
Come, Dietrich. Evidence. Evidence.

Dietrich takes off wire-rimmed glasses, and begins cleaning
lenses with tissue.

                    DIETRICH
          (kindly, after pause)
Well, consider. You love Hans' sister, do you
not?

Dietrich nods toward punch table, where Boy, 5, reaches for
more punch, Boy, 9, steps in to help, and Boy, 7, gulps
down a glassful.

                    KARL-FRIEDRICH
          (laughing)
Of course.

                    DIETRICH
And Hans and Gerhard here each love the
Bonhoeffer they have married.

                    HANS
Absolutely.

                    GERHARD
Most definitely.

                    DIETRICH
Well then ... is love any less real because it
cannot be SEEN?

                    KARL-FRIEDRICH
Ah, but you are wrong. Love can be seen!

                    GERHARD
No, Dietrich is right. We see the RESULTS of
love, but not love itself. Love itself is
nonmaterial.

Dietrich puts on wire-rimmed glasses.

                    DIETRICH
          But no less real than its material effects. That
          which we call love is evidence of the spiritual
          realm.

Karl-Friedrich ponders. Dietrich continues kindly...

                    DIETRICH
          In theology, we consider the WHOLE of reality,
          the material AND the spiritual, and are thereby
          one step ahead of the sciences.

Light LAUGHTER, smiles. Waiter offers sandwiches.

                    HANS
          Ah, Dietrich, open your eyes. The pompous church
          of Germany is totally out of touch.

                    DIETRICH
          Actually, I tend to agree. We'll just have to
          reform it.

                    HANS
               (sarcastically)
          Good luck!

                    FRANZ
          Never underestimate Dietrich.

Dietrich, surprised, spins around and breaks into big
smile. He throws an arm around Franz and brings him into
the group.

                    DIETRICH
          Franz! Thanks for coming! Gentlemen, Franz
          Hildebrandt. One of my better students.

                    FRANZ
          Come now, Dietrich!

LAUGHTER. Dietrich makes introductions.

                    DIETRICH

                    My eldest brother, Karl-Friedrich, professor of
                    Chemistry, and brother-in-laws, Gerhard Leibholz
                    and Hans von Dohnanyi ... both attorneys.

                              FRANZ
                    A rarity. We outnumber the lawyers ...

LAUGHTER.

                              FRANZ
                    ... that is ... until you leave on Sabbatical.

                              HANS
                    What's this?

                              DIETRICH
                    Yes, in America, actually ... New York.

DIETRICH'S FATHER taps knife against water goblet, his arm
around waste of DIETRICH'S MOTHER, both 50s. Crowd falls
silent. Young Bearded Man clearly visible in the
background.

                              DIETRICH'S FATHER
                    A few words, if you please, on this special
                    occasion. And, I promise, they will be few.

Light LAUGHTER.

                              DIETRICH'S FATHER
                    Congratulations to our Dietrich, now Doctor of
                    Theology.

Polite APPLAUSE. Dietrich acknowledges.

                              DIETRICH'S FATHER
                    May your keen mind and concern for others make
                    you a blessing to many.

APPLAUSE. Dietrich's Father grows serious.

                              DIETRICH'S FATHER
                    But my toast tonight is not for Dietrich alone.

We begin pan of following: CHRISTINE joins Hans and lightly
squeezes his arm.

                    DIETRICH'S FATHER
          Most of you represent a new generation in Germany
          ... one that will, I fear, encounter many
          difficulties. Communists clamor from the Left,
          National Socialists from the Right...

SABINE leans head against Gerhard's shoulder.

                    DIETRICH'S FATHER
          ... and conflict seems inevitable. Those who
          seek easy answers are drawn to their voices.

Franz is next.

                    DIETRICH'S FATHER
          My young friends, unless you step forward with
          the voice of reason, one of these extremes will
          surely gain the upper hand...

We end pan on Dietrich.

                    DIETRICH'S FATHER
          ... which will form a fist ... that will fall not
          only upon those at the opposite end of the
          spectrum, but upon us all.

Dietrich's Father proposes toast.

                    DIETRICH'S FATHER
          May we here resolve to be used of your God,
          Dietrich, to save our nation from such
          catastrophe.

All raise glasses.

                    DIETRICH'S FATHER
          A toast to our Dietrich ... and to your
          generation. May you be a blessing to our nation.

Glasses clink amid clamor of HEAR, HEAR as all drink to
toast. General discussion resumes, and Dietrich says to
Franz and Gerhard...

                    DIETRICH
          By the way, you two have something in common.
          Your mothers are Jewish.

LOUD MARCHING OF SOLDIERS, then begin MOVIE THEME.

EXT. SHIP AT SEA - DAY

Ocean liner slips through calm sea. SEAGULLS call, waves
SPLASH. LOW MOAN of ship's horn. Dietrich leans on
railing, looking out to sea; talks and laughs (silent to
us) in small group seated on deck; buys ice cream for
children, whose parents beam with gratitude; plays piano
around which children and adults stand and sing (silent to
us); and observes the Statue of Liberty up close in
passing. He takes off wire-rimmed glasses to clean lenses.
"NEW YORK" fades in/out screen center.

EXT. SHIP AT DOCK - DAY

Dietrich carries bags down ramp and past newspaper stand,
not noticing headline: "COMMUNISTS AND NAZIS INCREASE SEATS
IN REICHSTAG". MOVIE THEME ENDS.

EXT. SEMINARY BUILDING - DAY

Students scurry about. Dietrich and FRANK, 20s, a black
student, converse as they exit building and proceed down
sidewalk.

                    FRANK
          I'm tired of all this highfalutin talk.

                    DIETRICH
          What do you mean?

                    FRANK
          The contest in there to contrive the most
          convoluted, abstract, useless, religiously
          esoteric statement possible.

Both LAUGH.

                    DIETRICH
          I know what you mean.

                    FRANK
          Theologians do no one any good.

                    DIETRICH
                 (surprised)

What?

                    FRANK
          Dietrich, it's not about theology. Theology's
          all over the map. It's about Jesus.

Dietrich listens.

                    FRANK
          Listen. You want to be a theologian, fine. But,
          if you want to be a Christian, that's a different
          matter entire.

City bus pulls up. Dietrich gets in line to board.

                    FRANK
          You want to meet some people who still know what
          the gospel is?

Dietrich looks at Frank.

                    FRANK
          Just a small church in Harlem, 2:30 Sunday. I'll
          call with directions.

Dietrich starts into bus, stops, looks back, and calls
out...

                    DIETRICH
          But I don't drive.

INT. AUTOMOBILE - DAY

Dietrich rides in Frank's convertible, top down.

                    FRANK
          You don't drive?

                    DIETRICH
          I have never learned.

Frank cuts through traffic.

                    FRANK
          I'll teach you.

Dietrich glances warily at Frank.

EXT. HARLEM STREET - DAY

Cars parallel parked on crowded street. Frank and Dietrich
finish latching top on convertible as SISTER SMITH, 30s,
JAYLA, 13, JASMINE, 6, and GW, 3, come down sidewalk.
Frank makes introductions.

                    FRANK
          Sister Smith, allow me to introduce my friend
          from Germany, Pastor Dietrich Bonhoeffer.

Sister Smith smiles and extends hand in greeting. Girls
smile, GW gawks.

                    SISTER SMITH
          I'm pleased to make your acquaintance, Rev.
          Bonhoeffer. Glad to have you with us this
          afternoon.

GW stares at Dietrich.

                    SISTER SMITH
          These are my girls, Jayla and Jasmine, and my
          boy, GW.

                    DIETRICH
          Pleased to meet each of you.

                    JASMINE
          Mama, he doesn't look like a German.

                    SISTER SMITH
          Jasmine!

                    DIETRICH
               (laughs)
          What do Germans look like, Jasmine?

                    JASMINE
          I've seen pictures at school. They wear uniforms
          and funny hats.

                    DIETRICH
               (laughs)
          Not all of us.

LAUGHTER. Dietrich squats to GW's level. GW tentatively
rubs hand on Dietrich's cheek.

                    DIETRICH
          It doesn't rub off.

Dietrich picks GW up and holds him high in the air. GW
starts GIGGLING. Everyone LAUGHS. Dietrich and GW hug
each other. Dietrich sets him down and group continues
down sidewalk. People stream into storefront church
building.

INT. STOREFRONT CHURCH - DAY

Crowded. Single fan circles slowly overhead. Dim
lighting. Ragged piano missing ivories. Dietrich sits
between Frank and GW, who is still looking at Dietrich.
People fan selves. MINISTER, 60s, is speaking. Young
children move non-disruptively in crowd. Mothers give
attention while listening to Minister.

                    MINISTER
          ... and if a man comes into your assembly ... in
          ragged clothes...

VOICES track with Minister: "That's right" and "Uh-huh".

                    MINISTER
          ... and you say to him ... sit here in the
          back...

"Un-uh" and "That's wrong".

                    MINISTER
          ... and then a man comes in ... dressed in fancy
          clothes...

"Whew-ee" and "Lord have mercy".

                    MINISTER
          ... and you seat him right up front...

"Oh, boy" and "Un-uh".

                    MINISTER
          ... right in front of the preacher...

LAUGHTER, "Go on now" and "Look out".

> MINISTER
> ... close to the collection plate...

LAUGHTER, "Lord have mercy", "Un-uh", and "That's wrong".

> MINISTER
> ... how can you say that the love of God is in
> you?"

"Un-uh" and "That's right". Dietrich beams.

> MINISTER
> Or if your brother ... or your sister...

"Uh-huh" and "Say on".

> MINISTER
> ... is in need of food ... and clothes...

"Uh-huh" and "Lord have mercy".

> MINISTER
> ... and you say "Stay warm" ... "Be well fed" ...
> and then you go on your way...

"Uh-oh" and "Look out".

> MINISTER
> ... and you don't do anything ... to help your
> brother or sister...

Crowd into it: "That's wrong", "Un-uh", and "Lord have
mercy".

> MINISTER
> ... how can you say that the love of Jesus is in
> you?"

"Can't do it", "No way, preacher", and "Un-uh".

> MINISTER
> Jesus said ... "Do unto others...

"That's right" and "Preach it".

                        MINISTER
          ... as you would have them do unto you."

"Amen", "That's right", "That's what he said alright", and
"Uh-huh".

                        MINISTER
              Faith without works is...
                  (holds hand to ear)

"DEAD!" Followed by "Amen" and "That's right".

                        MINISTER
              Got food on the shelf?

Fewer VOICES: "Got some, pastor" and "Yes, sir". Dietrich
pans audience.

                        MINISTER
              Share it.

"That's right", "I will, pastor", and "Uh-huh".

                        MINISTER
              Got extra clothes?

Few VOICES: "Not much", "Sure do", and "Uh-huh". Dietrich
taking it in.

                        MINISTER
              Share them.

"That's right", "I will, pastor", and "Uh-huh".

                        MINISTER
          Did Jesus say ... steal what you need?

LAUGHTER. "No, pastor", "Un-uh", and "Lord have mercy."

                        MINISTER
          Did Jesus say ... get it from the government?"

LAUGHTER. "No he didn't", "No, pastor", and "Un-uh".

                        MINISTER
          Did Jesus say ... work with your hands...

"That's right".

                    MINISTER
        ... that you my have to give to him who is in
        need?

"Yes he did" and "That's right, pastor".

                    MINISTER
        And when you don't have a job...

"I hear you", "Uh-huh", and "Yeah".

                    MINISTER
        ... you've still got Jesus.

LOUD "Praise God", "That's right", "Thank you, Jesus", and
"Uh-huh". A few stand and CLAP.

                    MINISTER
        And when life gets tough...

We focus on Dietrich. LOUD "Oh, yeah", "I'm there,
pastor", and "Uh-huh".

                    MINISTER
        ... you've still got Jesus.

LOUD "Praise God", "That's right", "Thank you, Jesus", and
"Uh-huh". More stand and CLAP.

                    MINISTER
        And when the man is rough on you...

"Oh, my", "Uh-huh", and "I hear you".

                    MINISTER
        ... and he calls you names ... and treats you
        like a dog...

LOUDER "Lord have mercy", "Oh, pastor", "Pray for him", and
"Uh-huh".

                    MINISTER
        ... you've still got Jesus!

LOUD "Praise God", "That's right", "Thank you, Jesus", and
"Uh-huh". More stand and CLAP.

                    MINISTER
          And when they put you in prison...

"Save me, Lord", "Oh, no", "Lord have mercy". Close-up of
Dietrich at full attention.

                    MINISTER
          ... and when you got nothing...

"Tell us, pastor", "That's right", and "Preach it, pastor".

                    MINISTER
          ... YOU'VE STILL GOT JESUS!

CLAPPING and SHOUTING, "Praise God", "Thank you, Jesus",
"Amen", and "That's right". Everyone standing.

                    MINISTER
          I SAID ... YOU'VE STILL GOT JESUS!

Everyone standing and CLAPPING. Some hugging each other,
some arms stretched upwards. Dietrich smiles, CLAPS, and
looks around amid SHOUTS of "Praise God" and "Thank you,
Jesus" and "Amen" and "That's right". Minister tries to
calm them down.

                    MINISTER
          All right, now. Praise God! All right, now.

Audience calms somewhat, still CLAPPING.

                    MINISTER
          All right now. Praise God.

Clapping subsides and all re-take their seats.

                    MINISTER
          Life gets hard ... but we still have Jesus!

"That's right" and "Praise God!"

                    MINISTER
          Brother Louis. Sing us that song about Jesus,
          will you? It says it just right.

BROTHER LOUIS, 70s, gets up slowly.

> BROTHER LOUIS
> Sure will, pastor. Be glad to.
> (motions to pianist)
> Sister?

Brother Louis moves chair to front. Pianist takes seat.
Audience watches quietly. Children attentive, smaller ones
standing. GW climbs onto Dietrich's lap.

Begin Negro spiritual "GIVE ME JESUS" (Brother Louis
singing). Dietrich attentive and moved. Young Bearded Man
clearly visible in back row.

At conclusion, play UPBEAT SONG during following scenes.

EXT. HARLEM STREET - DAY

Frank's auto. Dietrich in driver's seat. Frank, in
passenger seat, gives instructions. Sudden starts, stops,
jerks. He swerves into trash can. People on sidewalk
LAUGH and take cover. Frank reaches over and steers back
onto street. Dietrich begins to get hang of it.

EXT. HIGHWAY - DAY

Sunny day. Dietrich and Frank sail down two-lane highway,
top down, bags in rear seat. They approach, pass, and head
into the distance.

EXT. DINER/PARKING LOT - DAY

Dietrich and Frank pull into gravel parking lot in front of
Southern diner. They enter. White Owner pushes Frank out
and points toward rear door. Dietrich starts to come out,
but is invited to stay. Dietrich shakes his head and
accompanies Frank to rear. White Owner hands Frank plate
of food through rear door, frowns at Dietrich, and shoves
plate at him, spilling food. He and Frank sit under tree,
shaking heads and LAUGHING as they eat.

EXT. HIGHWAY - DAY

Convertible heads down highway past sign, "Route 66".

EXT. ROADSIDE - NIGHT

Dietrich and Frank LAUGH as they struggle to put up tent in
wind and rain. Drenched, they sit under tree and eat from
tin plates, LAUGHING. Campfire.

EXT. SERVICE STATION - DAY

Dietrich and Frank back away from convertible, shaking
heads. Smoke pours from engine.

EXT. BORDER CHECKPOINT - DAY

Sign: MEXICO. Frank stands across border LAUGHING as
Dietrich tries to explain passport to Frowning Guard.

INT./EXT. TRAIN - DAY

Dietrich and Frank sit on moving train, looking out window
at Gulf of Mexico.

EXT. MEXICAN RESTAURANT - DAY

Frank vouches for Dietrich, enabling him to enter
restaurant. Workers eye Dietrich suspiciously. Dietrich,
speechless, shakes his head. Frank LAUGHS. END UPBEAT
SONG.

EXT. SHIP AT SEA - DAY

Ocean liner retreats into fog. LOW MOAN of ship's horn.
Newspaper in stand reads: "NAZIS INCREASE POWER IN
GERMANY". INCREASINGLY LOUD MARCHING OF SOLDIERS.

                                        FADE TO BLACK:

GRADUALLY INCREASING SOUND OF MARCHING SOLDIERS. "GERMANY"
fades in/out screen center, then "1932".

FADE IN:

EXT. STAGING AREA - NIGHT

Close-up of goose-stepping feet. Gradual pullback reveals
brown-shirted Storm Troopers goose-stepping down center
aisle to front of massive Nazi Rally with all the
trimmings.

BAND is playing rousing version of the "Horst Wessel Song",
which gets drowned out in following scene.

Close up of menacing eyes looking straight at us. Pulling
back, we see mustache, then face of Hitler, who ascends
from behind platform in front of massive Nazi flag.
GOERING and HIMMLER ascend several steps behind to his
right and left, followed by assorted cronies. Crowd
STOMPS, CLAPS, CHEERS, CLICKS HEELS, gives stiff-armed
salutes in odd directions, and SHOUT in unison "HAIL,
HITLER! HAIL, HITLER!". Hitler bounds to podium and
SHOUTS...

                    HITLER
          The German people! The German people! The
          German people! The German people!

"HAIL, HITLER! HAIL, HITLER!". Storm troopers wild-eyed,
awe-struck. Hitler raises arms and soaks it in.

                    HITLER
                 (shouts)
          President Hindenberg, it is time for National
          Socialism!

Massive CHEERS and SHOUTS, which then ebb somewhat.

                    HITLER
          The Social Democrats have failed! The Catholic
          Center has failed! The Nationalists have failed!
          And the Communists WOULD fail! President
          Hindenberg, it is time for National Socialism!

CHEERS, SHOUTS, with some catching on at end of refrain and
SHOUTING "NATIONAL SOCIALISM!"

                    HITLER
          Five governments in five years! Five Chancellors
          in five years! Instability, humiliation,
          unemployment, hunger...

Throng SHOUTS REFRAIN with Hitler: "PRESIDENT HINDENBERG,
IT IS TIME FOR NATIONAL SOCIALISM!"

                    HITLER

We have more votes than any other Party! We hold
more Reichstag seats than any other Party! We
have a better plan for Germany than any other
Party! We have a plan to restore German
greatness! ...

Hitler orchestrates with hands and crowd joins in refrain:
"PRESIDENT HINDENBERG, IT IS TIME FOR NATIONAL SOCIALISM!"

                    HITLER
          Now is our time! The others have failed! The
          future is ours! AND I WILL TAKE US THERE!

Massive crowd CHANTS with surprising unity, "HAIL, HITLER!
HAIL, HITLER! ..."

Hitler raises arms and soaks it in. Goering and Himmler
CLAP and LAUGH to his right and left, as Hitler says...

                    HITLER
          Ah, Democracy!

                    GOERING
          What did you say, my Leader?

                    HITLER
          Democracy! Sweet, foolish, partisan Democracy!
          You have served us well! We now bid you ...
          farewell!

LAUGHTER. Crowd continues "HAIL, HITLER! HAIL, HITLER!"

                    HITLER
               (quietly)
          The Communists wouldn't be so foolish as to burn
          down the Reichstag, would they?

They LAUGH UPROARIOUSLY. Crowd continues CHANT. We zero
in on Hitler's eyes, which dissolve into those of a
dragonfly.

INT. HALLWAY - DAY

Pulling back from close-up of clerical collar, we see
Minister taking last draught on cigarette before crushing
it underfoot. He opens door to reveal large meeting room
full of pastors.

INT. MEETING ROOM - DAY

MULLER, 50s, is speaking at Floor Microphone One.

                    MULLER
          I can hardly contain my excitement, Brothers!
          GOD is afoot in Germany!

Dietrich and Franz, seated nearby, are troubled.

                    MULLER
          Six million of our parishioners are unemployed!
          Many go hungry! The Communist menace is gaining
          strength! And all are demoralized!

MURMUR of agreement among throng.

                    MULLER
          But now ... GOD is stepping forth in answer to
          our prayers! GOD is raising up a Leader...

Dietrich and Franz clearly disagree.

                    MULLER
          ... who will create jobs, who will end the
          hunger, who will halt the Communists, and who
          will restore German greatness!

SHOUTS of "HEAR, HEAR!"

                    MULLER
          I speak, of course, of Adolf Hitler! None other
          than an instrument of DIVINE WILL!

Dietrich jumps from seat and heads to Floor Microphone Two.
VOCAL SUPPORT of Muller increases.

                    MULLER
          Brothers! Adolph Hitler needs our support! We
          would be wise to align with what GOD is doing in
          Germany and urge President Hindenberg to appoint
          Adolph Hitler as German Chancellor!

"HEAR, HEAR!" Dietrich motions for silence, then begins
speaking before it returns.

                    DIETRICH
          With all due respect, Rev. Muller, I must
          encourage the Brothers to strongly oppose this
          suggestion!

BOOS. Muller, still standing, casts angry glance at
Dietrich.

                    DIETRICH
          Dare we claim God's endorsement of one who
          employs such strong-armed tactics as does
          Hitler?!

Muller's expression changes to condescension.

                    MULLER
          Pastor Bonhoeffer. National Socialism is our
          bulwark against Communism ... which advocates an
          ATHEIST state!

Swastika-wearing pastors SCOFF at Dietrich.

                    MULLER
          Surely you would agree that God opposes atheism!

LAUGHTER. Muller smiles and continues...

                    MULLER
          Surely you would not think Satan to drive out
          Satan!

More LAUGHTER. Dietrich raises voice over laughter.

                    DIETRICH
          I reject Marxism, just as you, Rev. Muller.
          However we differ in that I believe God is not to
          be found at EITHER extreme ... the Right OR the
          Left!

Muller frowns. A few shout "HEAR, HEAR"!

                    DIETRICH
          And Satan CAN disguise himself as an angel of
          light ... not that the Nazis are LIGHT by any
          means.

Some LAUGHTER, but most PROTEST.

                    MULLER
              (wagging finger)
          Careful, young one, careful. Labeling as being
          from Satan what is actually from God is a
          dangerous business ... and not just with respect
          to the Almighty.

VOCAL SUPPORT from many. PROTEST from others.

                    DIETRICH
          Just such threats, Rev. Muller, make clear that
          National Socialism is NOT of God ... not by ANY
          stretch of the imagination!

SHOUTS of "HEAR, HEAR!" And "SIT DOWN!" Our focus shifts
to MODERATOR at Podium Microphone on large stage.

                    MODERATOR
          Gentlemen, gentlemen, please! Might not our
          wisest course of action be to take NO position on
          this issue?

MURMUR of agreement. Dietrich and Franz aghast.

                    MODERATOR
          Our parishioners are variously aligned ... and
          unless we wish to alienate them, we would do well
          to avoid taking political positions.

MURMUR among pastors.

                    MODERATOR
          And remember. God graciously provides our
          salaries from the government treasury. Surely he
          would not have us jeopardize that arrangement.

Dietrich SHOUTS into microphone...

                    DIETRICH
          My Brothers! What is this? We are counseled to
          remain silent?! To not speak out against evil?!

Some "HEAR, HEAR!" Others, "SIT DOWN!"

                    DIETRICH

We are counseled to hold personal privilege above
denouncing evil?!

CHAOS. Muller fumes.

EXT. BONHOEFFER HOME - DAY

Address plaque, "Marienburger-Allee 43".

INT. BONHOEFFER PARLOR - DAY

Hans, Franz, and Christine gather around 1930s console
radio, which Gerhard is tuning. "February 1, 1933" fades
in/out screen center.

                    CHRISTINE
          Come, Mother. Dietrich is about to speak on the
          radio.

Dietrich's Mother and Sabine enter from kitchen. All
concerned.

                    GERHARD
          Is he still going through with it?

                    HANS
          You know he will.

                    SABINE
          But it's all over now.

                    HANS
          It's not over yet. Not by a long shot.

                    DIETRICH'S MOTHER
          But ... it IS dangerous.

They look at each other. Gerhard finds frequency.
NEWSCASTER is speaking in background...

                    NEWSCASTER
          ... to repeat: President Hindenberg...

                    HANS
          Quiet! Here it is again.

                    NEWSCASTER

>   ... has appeared Adolf Hitler as German
>   Chancellor and has called on him to form a
>   coalition government.

INT. REICHSTAG CHAMBER - DAY

As Newscaster reads, we see slow-moving, heavy-set, aged
HINDENBURG introducing and welcoming Hitler to Reichstag
podium. Hitler acknowledges cheers (silent to us).

>   NEWSCASTER
>   President Hindenberg cited the plurality vote
>   received by National Socialists in the last
>   election...

INT. BONHOEFFER PARLOR - DAY

Hans agitated. Newscaster's voice in background.

>   HANS
>   Von Papen cut a deal with Hindenberg ... appoint
>   him Vice Chancellor and he, the Nationalists, and
>   the Social Democrats will keep Hitler in check.

>   GERHARD
>   Fat chance.

>   NEWSCASTER
>   ... and the lack of opposition from the church...

INT. RADIO STUDIO - DAY

Glass separates Control Room from Studios A and B.
Engineer in Control Room, NEWSCASTER in Studio A, and
Dietrich in Studio B. Newscaster cups one hand over ear.

>   NEWSCASTER
>   ... in making the appointment.

Engineer readies to signal Dietrich, who puts on wire-
rimmed glasses.

>   NEWSCASTER
>   And that concludes this reading of the news. We
>   now welcome to the microphone, the Rev. Dr.
>   Dietrich Bonhoeffer, professor of theology at the
>   University of Berlin, who will speak on the topic

of leadership. The next voice will be that of
the Rev. Dr. Bonhoeffer.

Engineer points to Dietrich.

                    DIETRICH
          Thank you. I am most happy to discuss this
          timely topic with our radio audience today...

Clock behind him reads 12:05.

                                        DISSOLVE TO:

INT. BONHOEFFER PARLOR - DAY

Family huddled around radio. Clock above radio reads
12:15.

                    DIETRICH
          ... or is the current demand for a Leader simply
          a manifestation of juvenile psychology?

                    HANS
          Careful, Dietrich...

                    DIETRICH
          And if that is so, at what point does leading and
          being led become pathological and extreme?

Radio begins to CRACKLE.

                    SABINE
          What happened?

All listen, worried. CRACKLING. Silence. Suddenly, a
ROUSING RENDITION of the "Horst Wessel Song" begins to
play. We pan from face to face, ending with Hans, who is
fuming.

INT. RADIO STUDIO - DAY

A smiling Bruno stands with arms crossed behind petrified
Engineer, who looks helplessly at Dietrich. Dietrich
pauses, takes off headset, sits back in chair, picks up
text, and reads quietly...

                    DIETRICH

We must be clear on this point and cut through
all deception. Otherwise, our health may be in
jeopardy, for leaders can easily become mis-
leaders who set themselves up as gods...

Dietrich flips text onto table, takes removes wire-rimmed
glasses, and says...

                    DIETRICH
          ... thereby mocking God.

Bruno is not smiling.

INT. REICHSTAG CHAMBER - NIGHT

Storm troopers hurriedly pour gasoline onto floor.
"February 27, 1933" fades in/out screen center. Hands
illumined at strike of match. Torch is lit and thrown
through doorway. WHOOSH! Gigantic blaze erupts.

EXT. REICHSTAG - NIGHT

Reichstag ablaze. Windows EXPLODE. FIRE ALARM.

INT. BONHOEFFER PARLOR - NIGHT

Dietrich, Hans, Gerhard, Dietrich's Mother, Sabine, and
Christine listen to radio in dismay.

                    HITLER
          ... and so, to *protect* the German people against
          further Communist aggression, I am suspending
          certain constitutional guarantees of freedom ...
          until further notice.

                    HANS
               (mocking)
          And when might THAT be, my Leader?

                    CHRISTINE
          Hans!

INT. HITLER'S OFFICE - NIGHT

Hitler at microphone, with trace of smile.

                    HITLER

Temporary restrictions are being placed upon the
freedom of speech, of the press, and of assembly
... as well as regarding the privacy of letters,
telegrams, telephone conversations...

INT. BONHOEFFER PARLOR - NIGHT

SWAAAP! Hans pounds his fist into other hand.

                    CHRISTINE
          Hans!

                    HITLER
          ... the need for search warrants, and the
          prohibition against the confiscation of private
          property.

Dietrich's Mother turns to look at Dietrich. We begin slow
zoom onto Dietrich's face.

                    HITLER
          Those disobeying these safeguards will be
          arrested and given opportunity to reflect upon
          the seriousness of their behavior...

Close-up of Dietrich.

                    HITLER
          ... in camps set up to facilitate just such ...
          concentration.

Flash of sign on iron gate at concentration camp, the word
"FLOSSENBURG" visible for a split second. Hitler's voice
fades into background.

                    DIETRICH
          "Turning and turning in the widening gyre...

EXT. POLLING PLACE - DAY

Sign on window, "POLLING STATION". Storm troopers admit
voters wearing swastikas, but halt others and ask for ID.
We hear Dietrich's voice as Troopers smile while Person
fumbles for ID. Trooper examines, shakes head, and motions
for person to leave. Person protests, whereupon he is
shoved away violently by LAUGHING Storm troopers.

                    DIETRICH
          ... the falcon cannot hear the falconer; things
          fall apart; the centre cannot hold; mere anarchy
          is loosed upon the world...

EXT. STREET SCENE - NIGHT

Storm troopers fight citizens on the streets. SIRENS.

                    DIETRICH
          ... the blood-dimmed tide is loosed, and
          everywhere the ceremony of innocence is
          drowned...

INT. MEETING ROOM - DAY

Flashback to Moderator counseling pastors to neutrality.

                    DIETRICH
          ... the best lack all convictions...

EXT. STAGING AREA - NIGHT

Flashback to Hitler shouting from podium.

                    DIETRICH
          ... while the worst are full of passionate
          intensity."

                                        DISSOLVE TO:

EXT. SHOP OF JEWISH PERSON - DAY

Storm trooper and partner with machine gun guard entry into
shop. Dietrich's Mother and GRANDMA BONHOEFFER, 90,
approach. "April 1, 1933" fades in/out screen center.

                    HITLER
          Our fight against the Communist Jew is strictly
          self-defense! My fellow Germans, I urge you to
          boycott all Jewish shops ... THEN the Jew will
          see what he is up against!

Trooper casually bars entrance. He is gently pushed aside
by Grandma's folded umbrella.

                    GRANDMA BONHOEFFER

                    Excuse me, please.

                         STORM TROOPER
              I can't vouch for your safety in there, Granny.

Dietrich's Mother and Grandma enter shop and are welcomed
by Young Bearded Man.

INT. SHOP - DAY

Young Bearded Man gently reaches out, intending to take
Grandma's hands in welcome.

                         YOUNG BEARDED MAN
                    Bless you, Julie.

She acknowledges him absentmindedly while looking back at
Troopers. Hearing call of CLERK, she walks in her
direction, then casts puzzled look toward Young Bearded Man
O.S.

                         CLERK
                    Grandma Bonhoeffer, Paula. Thank you. How can I
                    help you today?

EXT. SHOP OF JEWISH PERSON - DAY

Grandma and Dietrich's Mother exit shop, packages in hand.
Storm trooper taunts...

                         STORM TROOPER
                    Bonhoeffer. Seems like I've heard that name
                    somewhere before.

Grandma stops. Trooper attempts to push packages out of
Grandma's arms. Grandma turns away, hands package to
Dietrich's Mother, and then does 360 (as fast as she can,
but she's 90) attempting to whack Trooper in gut with
closed umbrella. He calmly grabs it before it can strike.
His partner points machine gun at Grandma. Troopers LAUGH
as the first flings Grandma's umbrella far down the
sidewalk.

                         STORM TROOPER
                    Beat it, Granny, before you get hurt.

Young Bearded Man watches sadly through shop window.

INT. MEETING ROOM - DAY

Room is packed with clerical-collared pastors, many wearing
swastikas. Dietrich stands at Floor Microphone Two
speaking. Franz is seated just beneath him.

                    DIETRICH
          Brothers! The Aryan Paragraph before us today is
          unconscionable! Excluding Christians of Jewish
          descent from the church is absurd! The entire
          early church was Jewish, Paul was Jewish, the
          disciples were Jewish, JESUS was Jewish!

Franz tense. Swastika-wearing pastors fume. Muller rises
and heads to Floor Microphone One.

                    DIETRICH
          And such discrimination against the Jewish people
          would become official policy were we to endorse
          Hitler's effort to establish one national Reich
          Church!

Muller interrupts and speaks condescendingly.

                    MULLER
          My dear, young, Rev. Bonhoeffer ... you are sooo
          ... short-sighted.
               (to assembly)
          Think of it, my Brothers! Our Leader, Adolf
          Hitler, wanting to create a Germany conscious of
          belief in God!

Some SHOUT, "HEAR, HEAR!" Others, "NO!"

                    MULLER
          The State opening its arms to the church, wanting
          to protect it, to promote it, to purify it! Only
          a FOOL would fail to see the hand of God in this!

SHOUTS of "HEAR, HEAR!" And "NO!".

                    DIETRICH
               (shouts)
          God is no more in league with National Socialism
          than he is with the Devil himself!

Nazi Pastor jumps up and attempts to wrest microphone from
Dietrich. Franz rises to Dietrich's aid. Dietrich retains
microphone.

                    DIETRICH
                 (shouts)
            Not all Jewish people are Communists, just as not
            all Gentiles are Nazis!

Moderator BANGS gavel.

                    MULLER
                 (shouts)
            I would watch my tongue, young one! Many ears
            are listening!

Pastors SHOUT. Gavel BANGS. Nazi Pastor attempts once
more to wrest microphone from Dietrich, who holds on.

                    DIETRICH
                 (shouts)
            Do you really expect me to cower before the
            Gestapo and its' effort to enforce politically
            correct speech!

                    MODERATOR
                 (banging gavel)
            Gentlemen! Gentlemen!

Pastors SHOUTING. Nazi succeeds in wresting microphone
from Dietrich. Dietrich and Franz sit. Muller smiles.

                    MULLER
                 (condescendingly)
            My dear Pastor Bonhoeffer. You misunderstand the
            Third Reich.
                 (to group)
            Our Leader's goals are peace and unity, just as
            those of Christ himself. Adolf Hitler is the
            very servant of Christ in Germany today!

Nazi pastors CHEER. Dietrich and Franz flabbergasted.

                    MULLER
            And when you speak ill of the Reich ... you speak
            ill of Christ!!

Dietrich jumps up. Franz holds him back. Pastors unruly.
Some SHOUT "BRAVO", others "NO! NO!" Moderator BANGS
gavel.

                    MULLER
                (shouts)
        I call the question!

CHAOS.

                    MODERATOR
                (banging gavel)
        Sit down! Everyone, sit down! The question has
        been called!

All still standing.

                    MODERATOR
                (shouts)
        Resolved, that the pastors of Berlin do hereby
        support the Third Reich's establishment of one,
        unified, German, national Reich Church.

                    MULLER
                (shouts)
        Including the Aryan Paragraph...

                    DIETRICH
                (shouts)
        NO!

                    MODERATOR
        ... including the Aryan Paragraph! All in favor?

Thunderous SHOUT of "AYE" from Nazi Pastors.

                    MODERATOR
        Opposed?

Dietrich, Franz, and minority SHOUT "NAY".

                    MODERATOR
                (bangs gavel)
        The resolution is adopted!

Nazi pastors CHEER, shake each others hands, slap each
other on back, and LAUGH at Dietrich and Franz.

                    DIETRICH
                  (to Franz)
        It comes by the democratic vote of clerics!?

Young Bearded Man sits in front row gazing sadly into
space.

                    DIETRICH
                  (agitated)
        Franz! Merely binding up victims caught beneath
        the wheel will not do ... we must halt the wheel
        itself!

INT. MEETING ROOM - DAY

Pastors gather around table, signing document. Dietrich's
name clearly visible as first, bold signature. "July 6,
1933" fades in/out screen center.

INT. HITLER'S OFFICE - DAY

Hindenburg, in military uniform, hands document to Hitler.
Both are standing. Hindenburg frowns.

                    HINDENBURG
        A protest. Berlin pastors. Over one hundred.
        Are you sure you are doing the right thing?

Hitler glances at document and causally tosses it onto
desk. Dietrich's name clearly visible. Hitler smiles.

                    HITLER
        That depends on what the meaning of the word
        "right" is, General. It's all relative.

Hindenburg frowns.

                    HITLER
        What do you say I let the people VOTE for Reich
        Bishop? Now, that be fair, wouldn't it?

Hindenburg brightens. Hitler distracts his thought.

                    HITLER
        Show me again, General. How is it? What is the
        correct way to march?

Hindenburg gets serious, snaps to attention, and begins
demonstrating march. Hitler smiles.

                        HINDENBURG
              Shoulders thus! Arms tight! Begin...

Hindenburg marches in place. He looks at Hitler. Hitler
begins marching in place.

                        HINDENBURG
                  Hup! Hup! Hup...

EXT. BONHOEFFER HOME - DAY

Address plaque, "Marienburger-Allee 43".

INT. BONHOEFFER PARLOR - DAY

Duplicating machine WHIRS away. We catch glimpse of flyer
entitled "Candidate of the Evangelical Church. VOTE for
MARTIN NIEMOLLER". Dietrich, Franz, Christine, Sabine, and
Dietrich's Mother work feverishly, bundling and stacking
flyers. "July 17, 1933" fades in/out screen center.

                        FRANZ
              Giving the people a vote for Reich Bishop?! What
              ploy is this?

                        SABINE
              And with such short notice! Just a few days to
              print, distribute...

                        CHRISTINE
                   (interrupts)
              And the press is playing this as Hitler being
              fair!

                        FRANZ
              The Nazis CONTROL the press!

                        DIETRICH
              We do what we can.

Parlor door flies open. Gestapo Unit led by hard-nosed
ROEDER and Bruno begins confiscating flyers. Roeder snaps
off duplicating machine.

                         ROEDER
          Get everything! What they are doing is illegal!

                         DIETRICH
          What ... you can't...

                         ROEDER
          We can and we are!

Gestapo Unit begins carrying bundles of flyers out the
door. Family aghast and helpless! Dietrich fumes!

EXT. GESTAPO BUILDING - DAY

Dietrich storms up steps, flings door open, and enters.
Franz follows. Sign reads, "REICH SECURITY".

INT. HIMMLER'S OFFICE - DAY

Dietrich bursts through office door. Franz follows. Bruno
and partner stop them in their tracks.

                         DIETRICH
          We demand to see your superior!

                         BRUNO
          You don't demand nothing in here!

                         HIMMLER
          Let them in, Bruno. I thought we might get a
          visit from Pastor Bonhoeffer.

They pass and enter Himmler's office. He holds injunction
in one hand, while extending the other.

                         HIMMLER
          Heinrich Himmler. I don't believe we've met.

Dietrich doesn't offer hand.

                         HIMMLER
          I see.

Himmler flips injunction on desk in front of them.

                         HIMMLER

It's a legal injunction.

Dietrich it picks up and reads.

>   HIMMLER
>   Your flyer IS entitled "Candidate of the
>   Evangelical Church", is it not?
>   (condescendingly)
>   Tsk, tsk... Why, that might deceive some voters
>   into thinking that yours is the only evangelical
>   candidate. We wouldn't want to be deceptive,
>   now, would we?

Dietrich spins injunction back onto desk.

>   DIETRICH
>   You don't even know what 'evangelical' means.
>   Hitler hasn't the faintest concept of the gospel.

>   HIMMLER
>   (taunts)
>   Careful, careful. You ARE in Gestapo
>   headquarters. Risky, very risky.

Dietrich unfazed.

>   HIMMLER
>   Let's agree on a different title ... then you can
>   print as many copies as you wish, only ... you'll
>   have to start all over again. I'm so sorry.

Dietrich fumes at Himmler, who changes tone.

>   HIMMLER
>   (angrily)
>   I will arrest you or anyone else who dares to
>   violate this injunction! Got it?! I would love
>   to introduce you to one of our new camps!

Flash of sign on iron gate at concentration camp, the word
"FLOSSENBURG" visible for a split second.

>   HIMMLER
>   Am I clear?! Now GET OUT!

Dietrich doesn't change expression.

EXT. BONHOEFFER HOME - DAY

Address plaque, "Marienburger-Allee 43".

INT. BONHOEFFER PARLOR - DAY

We pull back from newspaper headline on table which reads,
"MULLER ELECTED REICH BISHOP".

                    DIETRICH
                (agitated)
          We cannot permit the illusion that Hitler's Reich
          Church is in any way connected with the Church of
          Jesus Christ!

                    HANS
          Dietrich, FORGET this church business. There are
          OTHER ways.

                    DIETRICH
          No, Hans.
                (idea germinating)
          We must make clear that there IS INDEED only one
          church in Germany and that it is NOT the Reich
          Church.

Hans shakes his head in frustration.

                    FRANZ
          What do you suggest, Dietrich?

INT. CHURCH BUILDING - NIGHT

Dietrich pleads (silent to our ears) with audience of
pastors while we continue to hear conversation in parlor.

                    DIETRICH
          We need signatures! No one can sit on the
          sidelines! We need the signature of every pastor
          in Germany willing to risk opposing Hitler's
          imposition of the Reich Church.

                    FRANZ
          RISK is certainly the right word.

INT. CHURCH BUILDING - NIGHT

Franz pleads with pastors (again, silent to our ears).

                    DIETRICH
          Franz, we are contending for the church of God!

Pastors crowd around table, signing document.

                    DIETRICH
               (excitedly)
          We also need a confession for our times ... a
          clear statement of faith with which the Reich
          Church will be forced to agree or disagree.

                    FRANZ
          Yes! Their inability to affirm the basic tenets
          of the faith will reveal them for who they really
          are!

INT. BONHOEFFER PARLOR - DAY

Dietrich and Franz excited. Hans silent and frustrated.

                    DIETRICH
          The Nazis may have political power, but they do
          not have the truth ... and truth will win in the
          end.

                    HANS
          Can you be so sure? Your God appears to be on
          vacation, Dietrich.

                    FRANZ
               (to Dietrich)
          And who will write this confession?

                    DIETRICH
          Karl Barth?

INT. HITLER'S OFFICE - DAY

Hitler SLAMS document onto desk. "Pastor's Declaration"
clearly visible as heading. "October, 1933" fades in/out
screen center. Muller cowers. Goering observes.

                    HITLER

Another pastor protest?! I will NOT have
dissension! Can you handle your job or not, you
bumbling idiot!

Muller CLICKS heels and gives Nazi salute.

                    MULLER
          I am at your...

                    HITLER
          SHUT UP, you fool! All of Germany is falling
          into line except for this despicable little
          matter of the CHURCH ... of all things! Your
          task with these weak-minded people should be the
          easiest of all ... you imbecile!

Hitler shoves Muller.

                    MULLER
          My Leader!

                    HITLER
          SILENCE! There must be a thousand signatures on
          this document!

                    GOERING
               (calmly)
          Two thousand, My Leader.

                    HITLER
          TWO thousand! A protest from two thousand German
          pastors I do not need! Do you know what could
          happen should this spread among the people?!

                    MULLER
          Please, My Leader...

Hitler picks up document and begins to read.

                    HITLER
               (reads)
          "Pastor's Emergency League!" GOOD GOD! "The
          Confessing Church!" "The Reich Church has cut
          itself off from the church of Christ!"
               (shouts at Muller)
          How DARE you let this be circulated!
               (reads further)

"The choice before us is this: Germanism or the
Christian faith!" Who wrote this?!

> GOERING
> Top signature, My Leader.

> HITLER
> Bonhoeffer! Why do I keep hearing about this
> Bonhoeffer!

> MULLER
> (nervously)
> He's an agitator, My Leader! A young, fool
> agitator!

> HITLER
> Well, monitor him closely or your head will roll,
> Muller! Do you know what it means for a head to
> roll?!

Goering smiles at timid Muller.

INT. MEETING ROOM - DAY

Large assembly of pastors. "May 31, 1934" fades in/out
screen center. Karl BARTH, 50, eminent Swiss theologian,
reads at podium.

> BARTH
> "We stand together as a federation of German
> Churches, threatened by the teaching and actions
> of the party that refers to itself as the 'Reich
> Church'. We do not view ourselves as a new
> church body, but as the one true church in
> Germany, faithful to the Word of God."

LOUD SOLITARY BONG of church bell.

INT. CHURCH BUILDING - DAY

Franz stands to side of pulpit, reading to crowd.

> FRANZ
> "We confess that Jesus Christ, as attested to us
> in the scriptures, is the one Word of God which
> we have to hear, trust, and obey. We reject the
> notion that the church would have as the source

of its proclamation still OTHER powers, figures,
and truths."

Another SOLITARY BONG.

INT. BONHOEFFER PARLOR - DAY

Dietrich reads to his Mother, Hans, Gerhard, Sabine, and
Christine.

                    DIETRICH
          "Jesus Christ is God's assurance of the
          forgiveness of all of our sins, and has claim
          upon our whole life. We reject the notion that
          there are other areas in our life which would
          belong to OTHER lords."

SOLITARY BONG.

INT. HITLER'S OFFICE - DAY

Hitler, Goering, and Muller sit at table.

                    GOERING
              (reads)
          "The various offices in the church do not
          establish a dominion of some over others. We
          reject the notion that there should be some who
          are vested with certain ruling powers."
              (to Muller)
          That's you, Muller.

Hitler fumes. Muller nervous.

                    GOERING
          Let's see here.
              (reads)
          "We reject the notion that the state should
          become the single, totalitarian order of human
          life."

Hitler jumps from his seat, almost knocking Muller over.
He heads toward large window. Goering throws paper onto
table.

                    GOERING

They're calling it the "Barmen Declaration", My
Leader. And that's not all. I also have a
letter that Britain's Bishop Bell sent to church
leaders throughout the WORLD.

Goering picks up letter. Muller squirms. Hitler stares
out window. We begin slow zoom onto Hitler's eyes.

                    GOERING
          "A revolution has taken place in Germany that has
          affected the German church. The new Reich
          Bishop" ... that's you, Muller ... "has assumed
          unrestrained autocratic powers that are without
          precedent in church history."

Hitler's eyes narrow.

                    GOERING
          "Disciplinary measures taken by the Reich Church
          have made a painful impression upon opinion
          abroad..."

Goering pauses, looks at Hitler, then continues.

                    GOERING
          "... opinion already disturbed by the institution
          of racial distinctions which are wholly
          incompatible with Christian principle."

Muller cringes. Begin RUMBLING SOUND from Hitler's
direction. Goering glances at him and quickly summarizes.

                    GOERING
          It goes on to ask which should be recognized as
          the true church in Germany ... the Reich Church
          or the "Confessing Church".

Hitler spins around in a rage. He simultaneously draws
pistol from holster, SCREAMS, and FIRES over the heads of
Goering and Muller, who duck. Hitler lunges at Muller,
grabs him by the neck, and begins choking him.

                    HITLER
                  (shouts)
          You IMBECILE! Would the only international
          outcry against the Reich come from the CHURCH?!!

                         MULLER
              Help! Help!

Storm troopers rush through door and stop dead in their
tracks. Goering is smiling. Hitler pushes Muller away.

                         HITLER
              Get out! GET OUT! I will have NO opposition!
              NONE! You've had your chance! Now I will
              trounce the church! Get OUT, you fool!

Muller fumbles as he picks up papers, dropping some. He
decides to leave them lying and scurries from the room.
Goering LAUGHS. Hitler seethes and mutters to himself...

                         HITLER
              Bonhoeffer!

LOUD SOLITARY BONG of church bell.

                                          CUT TO BLACK:

FADE IN:

EXT./INT. HITLER'S OFFICE - NIGHT

As BRITISH BROADCASTER reads, Hitler stands at large window
of Chancellery, hands behind back, staring into the night.
We look up at him from outdoors, bottom right. He is
backlit, full height. We begin gradual 360 spiral up and
around Hitler, always getting closer to him (passing
through window at his right) until, at 330, we see his
stern face reflected in the glass. At end of reading,
Hitler's eyes suddenly snap to an angle that causes their
reflection in the glass to look directly at us.

Simultaneously during reading, we see superimposed images
of various Nazi activities: Storm trooper breaking down
door and FIRING machine gun; pastor being removed from
pulpit by Gestapo unit; classroom of children being taught
by swastika-wearing teacher; Storm troopers painting "Death
to Jews" on window of Jewish shop. Teletype CLATTERS in
background.

                         BRITISH BROADCASTER
              "This is the BBC. The grim events in Germany
              appear to be viewed with cynical detachment by a

populace desensitized by prolonged warfare
between Nazi and Communist. Hitler's elimination
of all opposition, even suspected members of his
Nazi party, seem to be taken in stride by a
nation whose people have been stripped of their
freedom of speech, where spies and informers
infest the land, where every man is suspicious of
his neighbor, where intense propaganda keeps the
people in a state of almost hysterical emotion,
and where the glorification of force and violence
has separated Germany today from other western
nations. This is the BBC."

                                        CUT TO BLACK:

Silence.

FADE IN:

EXT. CHURCH BUILDING - DAY

Storm troopers block entrance to Franz' church building.
Each has machine gun. Franz and parishioners upset.

                    STORM TROOPER
          I SAID there will be no service today! This is
          an unauthorized church! Now move along!

                    FRANZ
          We will NOT! You raid our files, steal our
          treasury, and now prohibit us from meeting?!

SHOUTS of outrage.

                    STORM TROOPER
          For the final time ... MOVE! While you still
          have your teeth!

                    FRANZ
          Do you just do as you are told?! Have you no
          fear of God?!

Crowd SHOUTS and moves as one in attempt to split cordon.

                    STORM TROOPER
          Arrest them! Arrest them!

SHOUTS, scuffles, running. All are captured, including
Franz, and forced into police wagons.

EXT. BONHOEFFER HOME - NIGHT

Address plaque, "Marienburger-Allee 43".

INT. BONHOEFFER PARLOR - NIGHT

Dietrich, Hans, Christine, Gerhard, Sabine, and Dietrich's
Mother are despondent.

                    HANS
          We obtained Franz' release with the help of your
          father, Dietrich.

Dietrich's Mother brings folded hands to her bowed
forehead. Sabine looks at Gerhard and then asks...

                    SABINE
          Do they know Franz is Jewish?

Gerhard and Sabine exchange glances.

                    HANS
          They know everything about everybody. Franz is
          lucky. A few days might have produced a
          different outcome.

The others are puzzled by his comment.

                    HANS
          I took Franz home, had him gather his things ...
          and put him on a flight to London.

Shock.

                    GERHARD
          You what?!

                    HANS
          Hitler is preparing a major move against the
          Jews, Gerhard.

Sabine puts head on Gerhard's shoulder. Gerhard puts arm
around her.

                    HANS
          Elimination of citizenship.
               (hesitates)
          Prohibition from marrying non-Jews.

Sabine CRIES quietly in Gerhard's embrace. Gerhard soothes
her.

                    HANS
          "Aryan" women under 45 prohibited from being
          employed in Jewish homes.

                    GERHARD
               (bursts out)
          What do they think we are?!

                    CHRISTINE
          It clearly reveals who THEY are.

Hans takes deep breath and speaks slowly...

                    HANS
          Execution ... if discovered to have had sexual
          relations with "Aryan" women.

All are silent. Tear rolls down Gerhard's cheek. He hugs
softly CRYING Sabine and kisses top of her head. Hans
frustrated.

                    HANS
          Where's your God in all this, Dietrich?!

Christine puts her hand on Hans' arm.

                    DIETRICH
               (replies after silence)
          Expecting those who claim his name to speak out
          against injustice.

Hans unconvinced.

                    HANS
          I'm not so sure about your God, Dietrich! But
          I'll tell you what! I am documenting every
          atrocity committed by the Reich! I am keeping a
          file. We will prosecute them some day!

Sabine and Gerhard look up. All are concerned for Hans.

INT. HITLER'S OFFICE - NIGHT

Hitler stands at 1930s map of Europe. "November 5, 1937"
fades in/out screen center. Goering, Himmler, General VON
FRITSCH, and assorted generals are seated.

      HITLER
    Gentlemen! We have arrived at a focal point in
    history! German lands have been taken from us in
    the past ... and now it is time to take them
    back!

Goering smiles knowingly. Von Fritsch troubled.

      HITLER
    We have a thousand-year history in these lands
    ... and a greater right to them than do others!
    The German people need room to grow ... more ...
    living space!

Hitler notices von Fritsch. He repeatedly SNAPS pointer on
map as he speaks.

      HITLER
    German-speaking peoples are currently separated
    by ARBITRARY boundaries ... Austria,
    Czechoslovakia, Poland! It is my divine mission,
    gentlemen, to unite our race under the Third
    Reich!

Hitler pauses and stares at von Fritsch. He turns back to
map and SNAPS pointer more forcefully on map...

      HITLER
    The Soviets are neutralized by our pact with
    Japan! The French by our pacts with Italy and
    Spain! And the British ...
      (laughs derisively)
    ... Chamberlain is a pacifist!

All LAUGH, except von Fritsch. Hitler confronts him.

      HITLER
    You don't seem pleased, General von Fritsch.

Von Fritsch looks at others and musters courage.

                    VON FRITSCH
          My Leader. Britain, France, and the Soviet Union
          have defense agreements with these nations. Our
          army is not prepared for such an undertaking. We
          will surely be defeated.

Hitler waves him off and repeatedly SNAPS pointer in hand.

                    HITLER
          Did they oppose our rise to power?! Did they
          oppose Mussolini or Franco?! Did they stop our
          rearmament?! Did they prevent us from retaking
          the Rhineland?! Will they ever enforce the
          Treaty of Versailles?!

Hitler BREAKS pointer in two with hands.

                    HITLER
          NO!

Generals stare at Hitler.

                    HITLER
          Will Chamberlain sacrifice British boys merely to
          prevent the unification of the German people!

He throws broken pointer over heads of generals.

                    HITLER
          NEVER!

Generals somber and silent.

                    HITLER
          Gentlemen! The sooner we strike, the better!

We zero in on Hitler's eyes.

                    HITLER
          Every generation needs its war. And I shall see
          that this generation gets ITS war.

EXT. BONHOEFFER HOME - NIGHT

Face of MARIA, early 20s. She walks down sidewalk with
FRAU VON KLIEST-RETZOW, 60s, who together turn up main
entrance, and past address plaque on brick pillar which
reads, "Marienburger-Allee 43".

INT. BONHOEFFER PARLOR - NIGHT

Dietrich's Mother, Christine, Sabine, MARIANNE, 7, and
CHRISTIANE, 3, are setting and putting food on parlor
table. Sabine takes napkin-wrapped silverware from pile on
rolling cart, hands one each to Marianne and Christiane,
and demonstrates where to place them on the table. The
girls are excited.

                    SABINE
          Place each one to the right of the plate, just
          so. That will be a big help to Mama.

Girls begin their task.

                    MARIANNE
               (quietly to Sabine)
          Where is Maria going to sit?

                    CHRISTIANE
               (loudly)
          She's going to sit next to Uncle Deetwick,
          remember?

Dietrich's Mother and Christine glance toward kitchen.
Sabine COUGHS loudly. Marianne turns to Christiane and
puts finger to mouth.

                    MARIANNE
          Shhh...

Dietrich pops head through kitchen doorway, Gerhard behind
him.

                    DIETRICH
          Did someone call me?

Simultaneously, Marianne, Dietrich's Mother, and Christine
say "NO" while Sabine and Christiane say "YES". They look
at each other in embarrassment.

                    DIETRICH

Let's take a vote. Who says, yes?

                    CHRISTIANE
          Meee!

Marianne looks at Christiane and puts finger to mouth.

                    MARIANNE
          Shhh...

Dietrich puzzled. Women go back to their tasks.

                    DIETRICH
          Something strange is going on here.

Dietrich's Mother and Christiane stop and look at him.
DOORBELL rings.

                    CHRISTINE
          I wonder who that could be?

Dietrich heads toward main entry.

                    CHRISTIANE
                 (loudly)
          It's Frau von Kliest-Retzow and...

Christiane is muffled by Marianne's hand over her mouth.
Dietrich looks back at them and opens door.

                    DIETRICH
          Ah, Frau von Kliest-Retzow. So good to see you.
          Come in. Come in.

They enter. Dietrich's Mother arrives at entry. Others
stand in parlor. Kliest-Retzow introduces Maria.

                    KLIEST-RETZOW
          Dietrich, you remember Maria. Maria is my
          granddaughter and a former confirmation student
          of yours.

                    DIETRICH
          I ... that was obviously some time ago.

Maria blushes. Kliest-Retzow smiles at Dietrich's Mother.
Girls GIGGLE. Dietrich's Mother grabs Kliest-Retzow's arm
and ushers her into the parlor.

                    DIETRICH'S MOTHER
          Come in, Ruth. So good to see you again.

Dietrich left with Maria.

                    DIETRICH
          I mean ... it's been a long time, Maria. How
          have you been?

                    MARIA
          Just fine, Pastor Bonhoeffer.

Christine and Sabine come up behind Dietrich. Girls run up
and stare at Maria. Christiane puts her arms around
Dietrich's leg, squeezes, and twists herself to and fro.

                    CHRISTIANE
          This is my Uncle Deetwick.

Dietrich stumbles a little and looks down at Christiane.

                    DIETRICH
          Not so tight, Christiane. I'm not going
          anywhere.

They LAUGH.

                    CHRISTINE
          Welcome, Maria. So glad you could come.

                    SABINE
          Dietrich, Maria is going to be attending nursing
          school in Berlin. Isn't that nice?

Dietrich, at a loss for words, is still being twisted by
Christiane.

                    DIETRICH
          Why, yes ... that will be nice.

All is a little awkward. Christine and Sabine escort Maria
into the parlor.

LAUGHTER around dinner table. Dietrich sits next to Maria,
the two girls directly across from them.

              KLIEST-RETZOW
Dietrich, if I may ... how are things with the
Confessing Church?

              DIETRICH
The universities remained closed to us ... as
well as licensure by the state. We are
attempting to train pastors underground.

Hans looks thoughtfully at Dietrich.

              DIETRICH
We haven't been discovered yet.

              KLIEST-RETZOW
That's quite a risk, Dietrich.

              DIETRICH
We must have pastors who are faithful to God ...
not to Hitler.

              MARIA
How did the church get into such a mess?

              DIETRICH'S FATHER
Weak people.

              DIETRICH
AND the wedding of church and state.

              GERHARD
Hear, hear!

              DIETRICH
           (to Maria)
Christians must be free to influence all aspects
of society. I fear for any nation where this is
not so.
           (to group)
But the official union of church and state is a
different matter, for then the state controls the
church.

                        GERHARD
          Let church and state be separate, but not God and
          state.

General agreement, "HEAR, HEAR". Dietrich's Mother rises.

                        DIETRICH'S MOTHER
          Well ... I have some clean-up to do.

                        CHRISTINE
          We'll help you, Mother.

All rise. Dietrich's Mother, the women and girls head for
kitchen, leaving the men, who sit. Hans grows serious.
Dietrich removes and begins cleaning wire-rimmed glasses.

                        HANS
          Dr. Bonhoeffer, what do you make of Hitler?
          Professionally, I mean.

                        DIETRICH'S FATHER
          Mentally ill ... carries that riding whip with
          him wherever he goes.

                        DIETRICH
          Yet the heart is capable of immense evil without
          the mind being insane, is it not?

                        DIETRICH'S FATHER
          I believe experience bears that out.

                        HANS
                (tentative)
          As Germany's leading psychiatrist, would you be
          willing to put into writing that Hitler's
          emotional state should preclude him from
          continuing in power?

                        GERHARD
          What are you driving at, Hans?

Hans looks toward kitchen and lowers voice.

                        HANS
          As you know, I am privy to certain information
          through the Ministry of Justice...

They look at him with foreboding.

                    HANS
          Hitler is planning to invade Czechoslovakia.
          Armed forces will soon be heading south.

                    DIETRICH'S FATHER
          The generals won't stand for it!

                    HANS
          Hitler will have no opposition. None. He
          defrocked von Fritsch for daring to question his
          plans.

                    DIETRICH'S FATHER
          Outrageous!

                    HANS
          Yes, but we may be able to stop him ... convene a
          people's court ... declare him unfit for office.

                    GERHARD
          That's quite a risk!

                    HANS
          Consider the alternative.
               (pause)
          And that's not all.

Hans looks straight at Gerhard.

                    HANS
               (regretfully)
          Jews will soon be required to have a "J" stamped
          on their passports.

                    GERHARD
          What now?!

                    HANS
          Hitler is serious about eliminating the Jews.

INT. LIVING ROOM - DAY

"September 9, 1938" fades in/out screen center. Dietrich
and Maria enter doorway and are welcomed by Gerhard,

Sabine, Marianne, and Christiane. Nanny nearby.
Christiane jumps into Dietrich's arms. Marianne hugs
Maria.

                    CHRISTIANE
          Uncle Deetwick!

                    MARIANNE
          Uncle Dietrich! Maria!

                    DIETRICH
          My little pumpkins!

                    CHRISTIANE
               (giggles)
          We are not pumpkins, Uncle Deetwick!

Marianne and Maria LAUGH. Dietrich nuzzles Christiane and
gives Marianne a kiss.

                    MARIANNE
          Are you coming with us to Wiesbaden?

Adults glance at each other.

                    DIETRICH
          Maria and I have been invited to join you on
          your picnic.

The girls CHEER and dance about.

                    SABINE
          Nanny, we'll be leaving shortly. Make sure the
          girls have everything. We will be back this
          evening.

Nanny and girls leave.

                    GERHARD
          Hans is certain, Dietrich?

                    DIETRICH
          Hans is certain. War may break out at any time,
          and after that there will be no chance of escape.

Sabine puts her arms around Dietrich.

                    SABINE
          Hitler would even separate me from my twin
          brother? When will I see you again?

                    DIETRICH
          In God's good time, Sabine. But for now, we must
          make haste.

EXT. LEIBHOLZ HOME - DAY

Two autos are packed for picnic. Girls are excited to be
riding in back seat of Dietrich's auto, top down, with he
and Maria in front. All drive away cheerily. Nanny waves.
Girls and Sabine wave.

                    SABINE
          See you this evening, Nanny.

                    GIRLS
          Bye, Nanny!

INT./EXT. AUTOMOBILE - DAY

Dietrich drives along highway, leading girls and Maria in a
HAPPY SONG. LAUGHING and GIGGLING.

                                        FADE TO:

INT./EXT. HIGHWAY - DUSK

Autos pull off highway. All are quiet. Girls know.
Sabine puts on brown jacket and fights tears so girls won't
see. She hugs Dietrich.

                    SABINE
          Why, Dietrich?

                    DIETRICH
          Sin and evil, a reality in this world ... but for
          us, not in the next.

He helps her into auto.

                    DIETRICH
          We do what we can, ask God's blessing ... and
          trust.

All are ready.

> DIETRICH
> (to Gerhard)
> Franz will be waiting for you in Cambridge.
> (pause)
> Be careful.

Girls teary-eyed.

> MARIANNE
> When will we see you again, Uncle Dietrich?

> DIETRICH
> In God's good time, my little pumpkins. In God's
> good time.

Auto pulls out. Dietrich and Maria wave.

INT./EXT. AUTO - DUSK

Girls look out rear window. Dietrich and Maria recede and
are cut from view as auto goes over rise.

INT./EXT. AUTO - NIGHT

Gerhard races along road. He and Sabine tense. Girls
quiet.

INT./EXT. CHECKPOINT - NIGHT

Girls feign sleep under covers. Gerhard pulls up to
checkpoint. Border Guard comes out and requests papers.
Gerhard gets out and provides. Guard eyes them, looks in
back seat, and sees sleeping girls. Gerhard opens trunk.
Picnic equipment.

> GERHARD
> Holiday to Basel. Should be back tomorrow.

Gerhard and Guard lock eyes.

EXT. BUILDING - NIGHT

We pull back from night view of lighted Eiffel Tower to gun
in hand of Figure in shadows outside of building on which
are illuminated the words, "GERMAN EMBASSY". "November 7,

1938" fades in/out screen center. German military officers
exit and stop in lamplight to light cigarettes. Figure
leaps from shadows, FIRES several shots into group, and
turns to flee. SHOUTING, CHAOS. Figure tackled and
brought back into lamplight. His head is forced into view,
revealing a wild-eyed teenager clutching a Hasidic hat.

EXT. STREET SCENE - NIGHT

"November 9, 1938" fades in/out screen center. Storm
troopers SMASH windows and torch synagogues and businesses.
Men, women, and children run in terror. YELLING,
SCREAMING, CRYING! They are roughed up and taken prisoner.
Repeated scenes of SMASHING windows.

EXT. STREET SCENE - DAY

Daylight reveals smoke rising from destruction. Broken
glass everywhere.

INT. HITLER'S OFFICE - DAY

Hitler, Goering, and Himmler agitated.

                    GOERING
          My Leader, the insurance companies are screaming!
          Property damage alone to synagogues, shops, and
          houses exceeds twenty-five million marks!

                    HIMMLER
          They cannot pay, My Leader.

                    GOERING
          And the life insurance...

                    HITLER
               (shouts)
          I don't care about the life insurance! The Jew
          must pay for his crime!

Long silence. Himmler brightens.

                    HIMMLER
               (craftily)
          My Leader. As punishment, require that the Jew
          relinquish all insurance monies to the state. We

take a cut, reimburse the insurance companies,
and they lose next to nothing.

A slow smile creeps across Hitler's face. He LAUGHS. They
all LAUGH.

> HITLER
> Excellent, Himmler! See to it!
> (pause)
> But I want MORE!

Goering attempts to one-up Himmler.

> GOERING
> My Leader. Levy a billion mark fine on the Jew
> ... as punishment.

Hitler LAUGHS. They all LAUGH.

> HITLER
> Yes! Yes! But I want MORE! The swine must
> never commit another murder!

Himmler attempts to one-up Goering.

> HIMMLER
> My Leader. Work the Jew in our camps until they
> pay off every last cent!

They LAUGH long and hard.

EXT. BONHOEFFER HOME - DAY

Address plaque, "Marienburger-Allee 43".

INT. BONHOEFFER PARLOR - DAY

Dietrich steams. His Mother and Maria are worried.

> DIETRICH
> I hear no outcry against these atrocities! No
> support of the Jewish people from our supposed
> "Confessing Church" pastors!

They try to calm him.

> DIETRICH'S MOTHER

Everyone is scared, Dietrich. These are
dangerous times.

                    DIETRICH
          Scared?! Where are the two thousand pastors who
          once signed our petition ... supposedly
          committing themselves to follow Christ at ALL
          costs?!

DIETRICH'S MOTHER
Men are weak, Dietrich. Talk is cheap.

                         MARIA
          "Cheap grace is the enemy of the church.
          Justification of sin without justification of the
          sinner."

Dietrich calms down.

                    DIETRICH
          You've been reading my books.

Maria smiles and puts her hand on his shoulder.

                    MARIA
          The final chapter hasn't been written yet.

Silence. Dietrich's Mother closes her eyes.

                    DIETRICH'S MOTHER
          Dietrich. Your year is being called up for
          conscription.

Dietrich looks at Mother.

                    DIETRICH'S MOTHER
          Could you fight for Hitler?

Maria closes her eyes.

                    DIETRICH
          Fight for Hitler? I wouldn't kill a flea for
          Hitler.

                    DIETRICH'S MOTHER
          What are you going to do?

Silence for some time.

                    MARIA
          Dietrich, might you get a deferment to teach at
          that seminary in America ... in New York?

Dietrich takes her by the hand.

                    DIETRICH
          Maria. I just lamented that the church isn't
          involved in the Jewish struggle. I can't leave
          Germany.

                    MARIA
          The Nazis are just waiting for you to make a
          mistake, Dietrich.

                    DIETRICH'S MOTHER
          Father's influence has its limits. What good are
          you to the Jews if you are in a concentration
          camp ... or on the front lines?

                    DIETRICH
          Or in America?

                    MARIA
          At least you will be alive.

                    DIETRICH
          Alive ... but tormented.

                    MARIA
          Really, Dietrich ... what can one pastor do?

Close-up of Dietrich's face as he ponders.

EXT. SHIP AT SEA - DUSK

LOW MOAN of ship's horn. "June 2, 1939" fades in/out
screen center. We pull back from Dietrich's face and see
him leaning on deck railing as Statue of Liberty passes in
background.

EXT. SHIP AT DOCK - DUSK

Dietrich comes down plank carrying baggage. Frank welcomes
him. They hop into Frank's car and head out. We see them
crossing 1930s bridge into Harlem.

INT./EXT. AUTO - NIGHT

Frank parks in front of storefront church. They get out.

> FRANK
> So let me get this straight. You came back to
> teach at that highfalutin seminary?

> DIETRICH
> Don't get me wrong, Frank. My theology is very
> practical. I wrote a book ... *The Cost of
> Discipleship* ... I should have sent you a copy.

> FRANK
> I've read it. Very good.

Dietrich surprised.

> DIETRICH
> I believe what I wrote. I used to be a
> theologian, but now I am a Christian. You played
> a part in that transition, you may recall.

> FRANK
> I remember. Then why are you here?

> DIETRICH
> What do you mean?

They enter the building.

INT. STOREFRONT CHURCH - NIGHT

Frank turns on singular light under slow-moving ceiling
fan. Piano with missing ivories in view.

> FRANK
> "When God calls a man, he bids him come and die."

> DIETRICH
> A quote from my book.

Frank is silent as they sit on folding chairs under fan.

                    DIETRICH
          I was speaking about dying to self. A person
          can't follow Jesus if he or she persists in going
          their own way.

Frank leans back, looking up at fan.

                    DIETRICH
          I've given my commitment to teach here at the
          seminary. I can't break my word!

Silence.

                    DIETRICH
          So am I to allow myself to be drafted into
          Hitler's army, go to the front, kill my fellow
          Christians, and die in the process?

Frank looks at Dietrich.

                    DIETRICH
          Am I to allow myself to be silenced in a
          concentration camp?

Frank sits up.

                    FRANK
          I don't know, Dietrich. But I do know that God
          has placed me where I am ... and that he expects
          me to do what I can, as a Christian, to eliminate
          the injustice around me.

                    DIETRICH
          But, Frank, it's different in Germany.
          Confessing Church pastors are either pledging
          their allegiance to Hitler, being sent to the
          front, or being silenced in the camps!

Frank leans back again, looking up at fan.

                    FRANK
          "When God calls a man..."

Silence.

                    DIETRICH

But what can I do?

                    FRANK
          God will show you, won't he?

Dietrich looks at piano. Begin partial REPRISE, "GIVE ME
JESUS" (piano only).

                    FRANK
          What is faith, anyway? Intellectual assent to a
          bunch of doctrines?

                    DIETRICH
          Faith is trusting God.

                    FRANK
          Is our goal to live long lives or to make a
          difference while we are here?

Dietrich sighs. Dietrich removes and begins cleaning wire-
rimmed glasses.

                    FRANK
          "Only the believer is obedient; only the obedient
          believe."

                    DIETRICH
          My book.

                    FRANK
          "Disciples take upon themselves what others
          conveniently shake off."

                    DIETRICH
          You have a good memory.

                    FRANK
          "Christ's life on earth is not finished; he lives
          on in the lives of those who follow him."

Dietrich puts on wire-rimmed glasses.

                    DIETRICH
          You can stop.
               (pause)
          You are right, Frank. You are right.

                          FRANK
           No ... YOU are right, Dietrich.

EXT. SHIP AT SEA - NIGHT

"July 7, 1939" fades in/out screen center. Dietrich leans
on railing as ship recedes from New York harbor. Full moon
rides above skyscrapers in 1939 New York skyline. Night
clouds sail. Ship recedes into darkness. End partial
REPRISE. LOW MOAN of ship's horn.

                                        FADE TO BLACK:

Increasingly loud CREAKING of tank tracks, until deafening.

FADE IN:

EXT. BATTLEFIELD - DAY

Panoramic view. "POLAND" fades in/out screen center,
followed by "September 1, 1939". Broad front of advancing
German tanks followed by massive numbers of soldiers.
Switching to German Troops' perspective, we see a line of
Polish soldiers cresting hill on horseback. Tanks BLAST
cavalry, which disappears over the hill. Topping hill, we
see ill-equipped Polish army and hear BLAST of German
tanks. Massacre.

EXT. TOWN/ROAD - DAY

German Troops herd Polish citizens from homes onto waiting
trucks, which form long convoy heading down road.

EXT. CONCENTRATION CAMP - DUSK

German Troops unload Polish citizens inside barbed-wire
fence. Young Bearded Man emotional as he tries to ease the
burdens of bewildered entering camp.

EXT. BONHOEFFER HOME - NIGHT

Address plaque, "Marienburger-Allee 43".

INT. BONHOEFFER PARLOR - NIGHT

Dietrich opens main door. Hans, General BECK, 60s, General
OSTER, 50s, and Stauffenberg enter.

                    HANS
          Gentlemen. May I introduce my brother-in-law,
          Dietrich Bonhoeffer.

All shake hands in turn.

                    HANS
          Dietrich, this is General Ludwig Beck, Hitler's
          former Chief of Staff; General Hans Oster, number
          two at Counter-Intelligence; and Colonel Claus
          von Stauffenberg, attaché to General Helmut
          Treskow, a member of Hitler's inner circle.

Dietrich impressed.

                    DIETRICH
          Come in, gentlemen, come in. Have a seat.

Dietrich's Mother and Maria enter with coffee pot and cups.

                    DIETRICH
          Gentlemen, my mother, and Maria ... a friend of
          the family.

The men acknowledge. Dietrich's and Maria's eyes smile at
each other. Beck flops down, agitated.

                    BECK
          We wouldn't be in this predicament were it not
          for Chamberlain and his accursed Munich Pact!

                    HANS
          Rose-colored glasses... We move on.

                    OSTER
          Hitler would be behind bars.

                    STAUFFENBERG
          Austria, Czechoslovakia, Poland, Belgium,
          Netherlands, France would be free.

                    DIETRICH
          As would the Jewish people ... and the church.

Dietrich's Mother and Maria look for a favorable response
to Dietrich's comment.

                    BECK
              (gruffly)
         Bonhoeffer! Each has his own perspective! Mine
         is strictly to avoid the military defeat of
         Germany!

                    OSTER
         We are sympathetic to your concerns, Dietrich,
         but we are military men.

                    DIETRICH
         Of course.

                    HANS
         Gentlemen. The past is past. The question is:
         what can we do about the future?

                    BECK
         Britain will never give the necessary assurances
         now that we have initiated hostilities!

                    HANS
         But we must try.

He turns to Dietrich.

                    HANS
         Dietrich, we are wondering if you would initiate
         contact through your Swiss ecumenical ties.

                    BECK
         Military intelligence works with everyone ...
         Communists, Jews, Poles ... why not Confessing
         Church pastors?

Beck LAUGHS.

                    OSTER
         As a Counter-Intelligence agent, Dietrich, you
         would be deferred from call-up ... and no longer
         be required to report your whereabouts to the
         Gestapo.

                    HANS

                    Internal politics, Dietrich. Counter-
                    Intelligence and the Gestapo are at odds: they
                    suspect us, we detest them.

Dietrich looks at Mother and Maria, then replies...

                              DIETRICH
                    I am ready to be used of God to stop Hitler ...
                    although it may prevent me from taking up my
                    ministry later.

Women concerned.

EXT. BORDER CHECKPOINT - DAY

Dietrich hands visa to Border Guard. "February 24, 1941"
fades in/out screen center. Guard examines it and studies
Dietrich. Visa reads "Counter-Intelligence". Border Guard
hands it back and allows him to pass. Sign reads,
"SWITZERLAND".

EXT. FLOWER GARDEN - DAY

Dietrich walks with Barth in quiet garden.

                              DIETRICH
                    Dr. Barth, Britain simply must differentiate
                    between Germany and Nazism. Many Germans are
                    appalled at what is being done in the name of our
                    nation!

                              BARTH
                    Given the atrocities in Poland and elsewhere,
                    that would be a hard sell.

                              DIETRICH
                    I understand. But they must be made aware that
                    we want to arrest Hitler and bring him to
                    justice. The coup cannot take place until those
                    involved are certain that Britain will negotiate
                    with the Resistance.

Barth noncommittal.

                              BARTH
                    Tell me, Dietrich. How do you, as a pastor,
                    reconcile giving the appearance of working for

Nazi Counter-Intelligence while actually working
for the Resistance?

Dietrich smiles.

                    BARTH
          Surely such an arrangement must entail a web of
          deceit ... layer upon layer of lies, compromise,
          cover-up ... and possibly even murder.

                    DIETRICH
          Dr. Barth, we don't want to murder Hitler ...
          just arrest him, convict him, and end this
          madness.

Barth unconvinced.

                    DIETRICH
          Hitler personifies evil. The longer he remains
          in power, the more victims, especially Jewish
          people.
               (pause)
          I simply MUST DO something.

Barth ponders. Long silence.

                    BARTH
          Tell me, Dietrich, for what do you pray in these
          days?

                    DIETRICH
          For what do I pray? I pray for the defeat of my
          nation. How else can we pay for the suffering we
          are causing the world?

INT. HIMMLER'S OFFICE - DAY

Close-up of Himmler on telephone with Oster.

                    HIMMLER
          Look, Oster! Counter-Intelligence handles
          military matters ONLY ... the Gestapo handles
          politics!
               (pause)
          No, I will decide the gray areas. I am much
          closer to Our Leader than you are. He'll side
          with me.

                    (pause)
          I would be glad to have you challenge me on that
          before Our Leader, Oster!
                    (taunts)
          By the way ... I am not unaware of certain
          irregularities within Counter-Intelligence.
                    (pause)
          What irregularities?! Like why is the pastor
          most critical of the Reich now working for
          Counter-Intelligence?
                    (pause)
          No, you listen to me! And why has Counter-
          Intelligence initiated so many deferments for
          Confessing Church pastors? Huh?
                    (pause)
          Oh, sure, sure. Listen, Oster! Something
          strange is going on at Counter-Intelligence ...
          and I'm going to get to the bottom of it!

SLAMS phone.

INT. HITLER'S OFFICE - DAY

Hitler stands at map of Europe, SNAPPING at locations with
a curled-up riding whip. Goering and Himmler present.

                    HITLER
          Poland ... Austria ... Czechoslovakia ... Hungary
          ... Netherlands ... Belgium ... FRANCE!
                    (laughs)
          And we've only just begun!

Hitler grows sinister.

                    HITLER
          Gentlemen. With the world distracted by war ...
          now is the time to purify our lands so that our
          people may live in them ... unfettered. It is
          time to *dispose* of the Pole, the Slav ... the
          JEW.

Goering and Himmler smile.

                    HITLER
          We ARE The Super Race of whom Nietzsche spoke,
          are we not? The Fittest of whom Darwin spoke?

Goering and Hitler agree.

                    HITLER
               (slowly)
          The Jew, the Slav, the Pole are parasites on our
          body politic ... and we have the right to do with
          our body as we see fit, do we not? Is it not
          simply a matter of choice?

                    HIMMLER
          Like flicking off a flea.

                    GOERING
          Nothing wrong with it.

                    HITLER
          Wrong? There is no right or wrong! God is dead
          ... like Nietzsche said.

They CHUCKLE.

                    HIMMLER
          Just do it!

                    HITLER
          It's nature's way ... the strong over the weak
          ... as Darwin did speak!

CHUCKLE. Momentary silence.

                    GOERING
          My Leader, before we ... dispose ... of them,
          might we, as the Master Race, first put them to
          use?

INT. FACTORY - NIGHT

Sweating, aching prisoners lug leaded balls, then heave
them into massive furnace.

                    GOERING
          Have them build our roads, toil in our mines, dig
          our ditches, sweat in our factories ... and then
          dispose those who survive.

LAUGHTER.

INT. CLINIC - NIGHT

Thin, fearful prisoner receives injection from white-jacketed physician.

                    HIMMLER
          My Leader. In the interest of science ... use
          them for various experiments ... like, exactly
          when does human flesh freeze ... how much
          pressure can the eyeball withstand ... at what
          dosage is typhus fatal?

LAUGHTER.

INT. BARRACKS - DUSK

Triple-decked sleeping quarters. Some prisoners lying
down, others standing, all thin, looking at camera.

                    GOERING
          My Leader. Waste nothing. Harvest the tissue,
          the parts, whatever, for commercial and
          industrial use ... soap, fertilizer...

                    HIMMLER
                 (interrupts)
          There's probably enough gold in those teeth to
          fill a bank!

LAUGHTER.

INT. HITLER'S OFFICE - DAY

Bug-eyed Hitler rubbing his hands together.

                    GOERING
          Make sure they bring their valuables with them
          for the "resettlement".

They LAUGH, then Hitler grows serious.

                    HITLER
          But if there are too many to manage ... simply
          liquidate them!

EXT. BUNKER IN FIELD - DAY

Storm troopers, machine-guns in hand, guard line of Jewish
People in open field. Bruno stands on top of bunker with
whip in hand. Machine-gun FIRE heard on other side of
bunker. Bruno SNAPS whip and orders next section of line
up and over rise, down into bunker. They go. Jewish
father, mother, son, and daughter wait third in line,
huddled together, hugging each other. Jewish grandmother,
second in line, holds and coos baby. Jewish father and his
small son are first in line at top of rise. The small boy
is staring straight ahead and CRYING. His father kneels to
comfort him and points heavenward. Machine-gun FIRE.
Bruno SNAPS his whip for next section to step down into
bunker. We rise above bunker and see the Gunman, cigarette
in mouth, sitting on clump of dirt, with smoking machine-
gun at his side. All is set. Gunman sets cigarette down,
stands, FIRES, sits, and takes another draw on cigarette.

                                          FADE TO BLACK:

FADE IN:

EXT. STREET SCENE - DAY

Machine guns in hand, Storm troopers escort Jewish men,
women, and children (each with yellow star sewn onto
clothing) out of their homes and into back of open trucks.
Neighbors watch.

                    STORM TROOPER
               This is Aryan land ... Aryan houses. Only one
               piece of luggage allowed. You are being
               "resettled".

Trooper notices Old Woman not wearing star.

                    STORM TROOPER
               Where is your star! Every Jew must wear a star!

She fumbles to get sweater out of her bag and hurriedly
puts it on.

                    STORM TROOPER
               Move along, move along!
                    (to all)
               Don't forget your valuables.

Overcrowded trucks roll down street.

EXT. TRAIN STATION - DAY

The masses are unloaded from trucks and onto waiting
boxcars.

                                        FADE TO:

EXT. BONHOEFFER HOME - NIGHT

Address plaque, "Marienburger-Allee 43".

INT. BONHOEFFER PARLOR - NIGHT

Conspirators converse. Dietrich's Mother and Maria listen.

                    HANS
          It's not resettlement. It's not detainment.
          It's extermination. Genocide. We have
          confirmation.

Dietrich's Mother covers her mouth, gets up, and leaves.
Maria stays.

                    DIETRICH
          In our own country ... the willful slaughter of
          innocent human life.

                    OSTER
          We must help as many Jewish people as possible to
          escape from Germany ... and quickly.

                    BECK
          Hitler must GO! He MUST BE DEALT WITH!

Prolonged silence. Hans turns to Dietrich.

                    HANS
          Dietrich... in what sense do you understand
          Jesus' words, "those who take the sword shall
          perish by the sword"?

Dietrich realizes implication. Maria worried.

                    DIETRICH
          He means what he says, Hans.
               (pause)

But might not our times call for those who would
risk taking that judgment upon themselves?

They look at Dietrich.

>   DIETRICH
>   Might not even a pastor be called risk his life
>   to save the lives of others?

Silence. Dietrich and Maria look at each other. Hans
notices Maria's concern and changes tone of conversation.

>   HANS
>   Let's start by getting as many Jews as possible
>   out of Germany.

>   DIETRICH
>   (enthusiastically)
>   That's EXACTLY what I want to do.

>   OSTER
>   But with great care! The Gestapo is watching our
>   every move.

Maria sighs slowly and deeply.

EXT. BONHOEFFER GARDEN - NIGHT

Dietrich and Maria walk in moonlit garden, hand in hand.

>   MARIA
>   I fear for you, Dietrich.

>   DIETRICH
>   Maria, God would have me DO something.

>   MARIA
>   You have a good heart.

They stop. Dietrich looks into Maria's eyes.

>   DIETRICH
>   I am simply a follower of Jesus.

Maria turns and leans head back against Dietrich. They
gaze at full moon.

                    MARIA
          I'm a Christian too, Dietrich. But do I do
          things that risk our future together?

Dietrich gently folds arms around Maria.

                    DIETRICH
          I love you, Maria ... but I love Jesus too.

Maria turns ear toward Dietrich.

                    DIETRICH
          We are his hands and feet, Maria. We are here
          for his purposes.

                    MARIA
          But would he bring us together only to tear us
          apart?

Dietrich gently turns Maria around and holds her close.

                    DIETRICH
          Maria.

He kisses the top of her head.

                    DIETRICH
          God would will us a long, happy life together.

Maria looks up at him.

                    DIETRICH
                 (tenderly)
          But he also wills that there be no wars, no
          injustice, no sin.

                    MARIA
          So his will is not done.

                    DIETRICH
          We pray that it is done, through us.

Maria puzzled.

                    DIETRICH
          God's will is of two types, Maria. When God
          chooses to act, none can stop him. But his moral

                    will must be obeyed ... and it is this for which
                    we pray.

Maria cuddles close to Dietrich, then turns around, and
they once again gaze at moon.

                              MARIA
                    You're right, Dietrich. Trust and obey. THAT is
                    God's will.

Silence. Maria turns and looks into Dietrich's eyes. They
gently embrace and kiss.

EXT. TRAIN STATION - DAY

Dietrich and Maria accompany CHARLOTTE along crowded deck.
"September, 1942" fades in/out screen center. Charlotte
wears yellow star on coat. Dietrich carries her bag. They
step away from the crowd. Dietrich shields as best he can,
glancing around while Maria discretely removes Charlotte's
coat and casually rolls it up.

                              DIETRICH
                         (quietly)
                    Remember ... only at the end. Karl Barth will be
                    waiting at the border.

Maria gives rolled up coat to Charlotte.

                              MARIA
                         (whispers)
                    May God be with you, Charlotte.

Charlotte receives bag from Dietrich and gets in line.
Dietrich and Maria stand back and watch. Porter takes
Charlotte's ticket. Train WHISTLE. She glances back, then
boards train.

INT./EXT. TRAIN - NIGHT

Charlotte sits on flattened coat, fearful, bag on lap. Her
image is reflected in window of speeding train.

INT. TRAIN STATION - NIGHT

Train stops. Passengers gather things in preparation for
disboard. Charlotte, nervous, puts on coat. Passenger A

casually turns around, sees star and gasps. Drawn by gasp, others stare at Charlotte. She looks away.

INT. BORDER CHECKPOINT - NIGHT

Passengers step in front of Charlotte, who ends up at very back of line. Her turn with Border Guard. Karl Barth is visible on other side of glass. She hands papers to Guard. He examines, then looks at her.

                    BORDER GUARD
          Counter-Intelligence, Jewess Friedenthal?
          Counter-Intelligence?

She glances at Barth, looks down, then at Guard. Guard locks eyes with Barth.

INT. COUNTER-INTELLIGENCE OFFICE - DAY

Hans on phone with Christine. Christine's voice is heard through receiver.

                    CHRISTINE
          Will you be late again tonight, Hans?

                    HANS
          I'm afraid so. Much to do.

                    CHRISTINE
          Shall we wait...

WHIRRR! Then MUFFLED VOICE.

                    MUFFLED VOICE
          Turn that off, you fool!

                    CHRISTINE
          Hans?

                    HANS
          I'm here.

                    CHRISTINE
          What was that?

Hans realizes they are being tapped.

                    HANS
          I heard nothing. Trouble on your end?

                    CHRISTINE
               (she knows)
          I guess not. I'll see you later then.

                    HANS
          Good-bye, Love.

                    CHRISTINE
          I love you, Hans.

Hans hangs up, rises, and gets Oster's attention with his
eyes. He steps outdoors and after a few moments is met by
Oster.

                    HANS
          My phone is tapped. I suspect my mail as well.
          The Gestapo's on us.

                    OSTER
          And the incriminating files?

                    HANS
          Coded and in the safe.

                    OSTER
          It's time to act.

INT. BARRACKS DINING ROOM - DAY

Oster, Stauffenberg, Hitler, Goering, Brandt, and several
others rise after lunch, conversing, LAUGHING. "March 13,
1943" fades in/out screen center.

                    OSTER
          Hey, Brandt. How about taking a couple bottles
          of brandy to my old friend, Helmuth Stieff. It's
          his anniversary.

                    BRANDT
          Sure. If I don't drink them along the way.

LAUGHTER. Oster and Stauffenberg glance at each other.

                    OSTER

                    Stauffenberg, where are those bottles?

                              STAUFFENBERG
                    I left them in the auto, sir.

                              OSTER
                    Assistants, what we going to do to them?

LAUGHTER.

                              BRANDT
                    What we do without them?

LAUGHTER.

                              OSTER
                    Get those bottles and give them to Brandt before
                    his plane takes off, hear?

                              STAUFFENBERG
                    Yes, sir. Right away, sir.

Hitler's party moves onto tarmac.

EXT. TARMAC - DAY

Stauffenberg hustles to limousine, picks up package, places
tweezers into small opening and presses. Bomb triggered.
He hustles to party boarding small plane. Hitler gets on,
followed by others. Stauffenberg hands package to Brandt.

                              STAUFFENBERG
                    Have a good flight, sir.

                              BRANDT
                    At least we have something to drink.

They LAUGH. Brandt gets on. Stauffenberg and Oster back
out of way, then wave as plane taxis and takes off.

                              OSTER
                    How long?

                              STAUFFENBERG
                    Half an hour. Silent. It's a two-hour trip.

They check their wristwatches. 12:45.

INT./EXT. AUTOMOBILE - DAY

Oster and Stauffenberg sit in auto listening to military
radio. Wristwatches, 1:15. They smile at each other.
Radio silent. They are puzzled. 1:45. They pull next to
telephone booth. 2:45.

                    MILITARY ANNOUNCER
          1475. Our Leader's plane has landed in
          Rastenburg.

Oster, panic-stricken, quickly exits auto, enters phone
booth, and dials number.

                    OSTER
          Operation Flash. Negative.

He hangs up, exits booth, reaches past Stauffenberg and
grabs military phone.

                    OSTER
          Brandt just might rip into it.

Oster dials.

                    OSTER
          General Brandt, please. This is General Oster.

They are scared stiff.

                    OSTER
          Brandt! Hey, hold those bottles for Stieff.
          Stauffenberg got things mixed up.
                    (pause)
          Yah, what we do without them?

He looks at Stauffenberg and rolls his eyes.

                    OSTER
          Stauffenberg is coming tomorrow on official
          business and will bring the right stuff.
                    (pause)
          Yah, I'll tell him.

Hangs up.

                              OSTER
                    Let's get you on that train, now!

He runs around auto, hops in, and PEALS OUT.

INT. WAR ROOM - DAY

Stauffenberg stands at closed door, package in hand. He
takes deep breath and opens. Hitler, Goering, Brandt, and
fifteen others are hunched over 18' x 5' table covered with
maps. Stauffenberg enters and all stop, turn, and look at
him.

                              BRANDT
                         (slowly)
                    Ah, Stauffenberg. We've been waiting for you.

Stauffenberg frozen. After a pause, Hitler, Goering, and
the others return attention to map. Brandt gets first
package. It is still wrapped.

                              BRANDT
                    You'll never make top brass if you can't take
                    care of the little things!

Brandt LAUGHS.

                              STAUFFENBERG
                    You've got that right, sir. Here's the good
                    brandy.

Brandt fumbles package with bomb. Stauffenberg catches it
with arm missing hand. He hands Brandt package of brandy.

                              STAUFFENBERG
                    Close call.

He looks at Stauffenberg, who stares back at him.

                              BRANDT
                    Loosen up, kid. It's only booze.

                              STAUFFENBERG
                    Sorry for the mistake, sir.

He begins to leave.

                        BRANDT
              You may succeed yet, kid.

Stauffenberg looks at him, then at Hitler.

                        STAUFFENBERG
              I certainly hope so, sir.

Brandt puzzled by response. Their eyes lock.

INT. RESTROOM - DAY

Stauffenberg enters restroom, carefully opens package,
unscrews bomb cover, clips fuse, and heaves heavy sigh of
relief.

EXT. BONHOEFFER HOME - NIGHT

Address plaque, "Marienburger-Allee 43".

INT. BONHOEFFER PARLOR - NIGHT

LAUGHTER and CONGRATULATIONS. Focus is on Maria's
engagement ring. Dietrich's Mother and Christine hug
Maria. Dietrich's Father shakes Dietrich's hand. Hans
slaps him on back.

                                            DISSOLVE TO:

Dietrich plays piano while Hans, Christine, Maria,
Dietrich's Father, and Dietrich's Mother sing. Clock
reads, 8:10. Slow zoom onto telephone.

INT. RESTROOM - NIGHT

Five-foot Colonel von GERSDORFF checks bombs in left and
right coat pockets. "March 21, 1943" fades in/out screen
center. Muffled sounds of "HAIL, HITLER" are heard in
background. Gersdorff pulls back cuffs to reveal wires
that run underneath each sleeve. He simulates wrapping
arms around imaginary figure, almost touching wire ends
together, and lifts hands quickly and makes "BLOOEY!"
Sound. He takes deep breath, puts hands in pockets, and
walks out of restroom.

INT. EXHIBITION HALL - NIGHT

SHOUTS of "HAIL, HITLER". Gersdorff pushes his way through
large crowd, looking for and trying to reach Hitler. He is
jostled here, stepped on there. Blocked in the press, he
watches his arms being forced together and struggles to
keep his hands from touching. He continues to struggle
forward, finally emerging in front of crowd next to
BYSTANDER, only to see Hitler entering limousine and his
Assistant closing the door.

>   BYSTANDER
>   I saw him! I saw him!

Hitler's limo pulls out. Dejected Gersdorff puts hands
back into coat pockets and stands silently as crowd
disperses.

INT. BONHOEFFER PARLOR - NIGHT

Slow pull-back from telephone. Clock reads, 11:00. Party
over. Dietrich and Hans are alone.

>   HANS
>   No phone call. Stauffenberg fails last week,
>   Gersdorff this week.

>   DIETRICH
>   I'm not altogether disappointed this time.
>   Gersdorff's a much bigger man than I am ...
>   willing to sacrifice his life.

Silence. Dietrich removes and begins cleaning wire-rimmed
glasses.

>   HANS
>   Speaking of bigger, Dietrich ... I would like to
>   believe in your God, but, tell me, if he exists,
>   why does Hitler succeed and we fail?

>   DIETRICH
>   Why does evil triumph?

>   HANS
>   Why, indeed?! Look who's running Europe: Hitler,
>   Stalin, Mussolini, Franco. Butchers all.
>   They've brought sorrow and death to millions, yet
>   our efforts to stop Hitler are thwarted at every
>   turn.

                    DIETRICH
          This is a fallen world, Hans. The evidence is
          all around us, even within our own hearts.

                    HANS
          So that's it? We're stuck? God cannot ... or
          WILL not ... do anything about it? What kind of
          God is that?!

Dietrich puts glasses on and begins to turn out lights.
Our attention is drawn to outdoor light streaming through
parlor window.

                    DIETRICH
          A God who doesn't force himself on us. A God
          whose revulsion of Hitler's actions is even
          greater than our own.

                    HANS
               (exasperated)
          Then why doesn't he DO something?

Dietrich and Hans walk to parlor window and gaze outside.

                    DIETRICH
          He has the larger picture. We do what we can ...
          and trust.

Hans frowns at Dietrich. Dietrich begins to make a diagram
on the humid window as he talks: rectangle containing C->E.

                    DIETRICH
          Listen, Hans. When God created the universe, he
          ordained that it operate in certain ways. Cause-
          and-Effect, for example. Join a sperm from
          Person A and an egg from Person B and what do you
          get?

                    HANS
          A new life ... unique person C.

                    DIETRICH
          Cause-and-effect. He also ordained Chance.

Dietrich draws Ch and an arrow from it to C.

                    DIETRICH
          Which of the millions of sperm is going to
          impregnate the egg? Is God sorting through
          millions of sperm a million times a day around
          the world for every human, bird, animal...

Hans LAUGHS.

                    DIETRICH
          Is he pushing forward the sickle cell gene or the
          Downs syndrome gene? No, Chance influences
          Cause.

Dietrich draws HC and an arrow from it to C.

                    DIETRICH
          And he ordained Human Choice. A mother who takes
          care of herself will normally deliver a healthy
          baby. One who abuses drugs and alcohol will not.
          Human Choice influences Cause.

                    HANS
          What's the point?

Dietrich gazes into the night.

                    DIETRICH
          Human Choice at Versailles created a climate
          where the evil intentions of Hitler fell on the
          susceptible ears of fallen human beings. Human
          greed and mismanagement created a worldwide
          depression, which Hitler exploited to his own
          advantage.

Their faces are reflected in the window, the diagram
between them.

                    DIETRICH
          Weak human beings failed to halt Hitler's advance
          at every stage. Did God want any of this to
          happen? No. But evil triumphs when...

                    HANS
                 (interrupts)
          I know, I know ... when good people fail to act.

                    DIETRICH

                    And the more it triumphs, the harder it is to
                    undo.

Dietrich looks at Hans.

                              DIETRICH
                    God doesn't force himself on us, Hans.

Christine comes up silently, and gently puts her arms
around Hans.

                              DIETRICH
                    Don't give UP on him, Hans. Give IN to him.

Hans studies Dietrich. Christine rests her head on Hans'
shoulder.

                              DIETRICH
                    Like Gersdorff, God was willing to make the
                    ultimate sacrifice ... except he succeeded. If
                    you'll turn to him and trust him, you'll succeed
                    too Hans ... no matter what the outcome.

Hans ponders.

INT. BONHOEFFER PARLOR - DAY

Dietrich dials phone number. "April 5, 1943" fades in/out
screen center. GRUFF VOICE heard on other end. Dietrich
assesses, remains silent, and quietly hangs up. He dials
second number. No answer. He hangs up, goes to desk,
takes out diary, flips to certain pages, gently tears them
out, throws them into fire in fireplace, and heads for
kitchen.

INT. BONHOEFFER KITCHEN - DAY

Clock on wall reads, 11:30.

                              DIETRICH
                    Mother, make me a large meal please.

Dietrich's Mother puzzled. His Father enters.

                              DIETRICH'S MOTHER
                    What is it, Dietrich?

                    DIETRICH
          A strange voice answered at Hans and Christine's.
          The Gestapo has been closing in on Counter-
          Intelligence.

                    DIETRICH'S FATHER
          You think they've arrested Hans?

                    DIETRICH
          And will soon be here.

                    DIETRICH'S FATHER
          What can we do?

                    DIETRICH
          Nothing, at this point. Just wait. I tried
          Maria. No answer.

Dietrich returns to parlor and tries again to call Maria.
DISSOLVE to clock, 12:30. Dietrich eating. KNOCK at door.
Dietrich's Father answers and returns to kitchen.

                    DIETRICH'S FATHER
          Dietrich, there are two men wanting to speak with
          you.

The three look at each other. Dietrich hugs his parents.

                    DIETRICH
          Keep trying Maria. Tell her to have faith ...
          and that I love her.

They go into parlor. It's Roeder and Bruno.

EXT. BONHOEFFER HOME - DAY

Bruno holds rear auto door open for Dietrich, who gets in.
Bruno gets in front, after which the black Mercedes moves
away slowly. Dietrich looks at parents standing on porch.
Mother's head rests on Father's shoulder, his arm around
her.

INT. PRISON CELLS - DUSK

Dietrich, in prison clothes, walks barefoot into 7' x 10'
cell. KNOBLOCH, a heavy-set guard, closes wooden door and
turns metal latch. CLANK! Dietrich looks around. Small

wooden bed, bare mattress, six foot high concrete walls
with bars above, damp concrete floor, stool, bench beneath
small barred window. In next cell, SCHMIDT CRIES and
MOANS. It's cold. Dietrich picks up thin blanket from
bed, is repulsed by the stench, and gently tosses it in
corner. He sits on bed, braces against the cold, rests
head against wall, and closes eyes. After a bit, he speaks
in low voice to Schmidt...

                    DIETRICH
          Friend ... do you want to talk? Can I help you?

Schmidt continues CRYING and MOANING. A prisoner,
HEINRICH, says matter-of-factly...

                    HEINRICH
          That's Schmidt. Never stops crying.

Another prisoner, KLINCK, SHOUTS...

                    KLINCK
          Shut up, Schmidt!

Dietrich flinches. Schmidt continues SOBBING.

                    HEINRICH
          Why were you arrested?

                    DIETRICH
          I'm not sure.

                    HEINRICH
          You'll find out ... although it may take some
          time to do so.

Dietrich glances up at small window. Dusk DISSOLVES into
night, then into dawn. Dietrich is curled up on mattress
against the cold. Schmidt still SOBBING. CLANK of
corridor door. Dietrich looks at cell door. Small
observation hole opens. A chunk of bread flies through and
lands on damp floor. After a bit, Dietrich says...

                    DIETRICH
               (softly)
          Hey, Schmidt. You want to talk?

                    KLINCK

                         (angrily)
          Shut up! What do you think you are, a preacher
          or something?!

                         DIETRICH
                    (quietly, to himself)
          Well, as a matter of fact...

Sound of prisoner getting off bed.

                         HEINRICH
          Not really, are you?

Dietrich gets off bed and heads in direction of voice.

                         DIETRICH
          Yes. Dietrich Bonhoeffer is my name.

Schmidt stops sobbing.

                         KLINCK
                    (contemptuously)
          Oh, great! Just what we need! A preacher!

                         HEINRICH
          Shut up, Klinck!

                         KLINCK
          I'll see you in the yard, Heinrich!

                         HEINRICH
          Yah, right!
                    (pause)
          Hey ... Schmidt is quiet.

Dietrich walks in direction of Schmidt's cell.

                         DIETRICH
                    (softly)
          Schmidt, you want to talk?

CLANK! Knobloch comes through corridor door.

                         KNOBLOCH
          No one is to talk to this prisoner! Those are my
          orders!

Dietrich's door swings open.

                    KNOBLOCH
          Prisoner Bonhoeffer, come with me.

                    HEINRICH
          Solitary. Sorry, preacher.

Schmidt starts SOBBING. Dietrich looks at bread on floor,
picks it up, and exits.

                    KLINCK
          Solitary! Ha! That's where all preachers should
          go!

After CLANK! Of corridor door, Klinck YELLS...

                    KLINCK
          Shut up, Schmidt!

INT. SOLITARY - DAY

Dietrich enters 5' x 7' concrete cell, tiny window near
ceiling, no bed. Knobloch shackles Dietrich's hands and
feet, sets in bucket, and closes door. CLANK! Dietrich
slumps against wall, slides down, and looks at light
streaming through window. It DISSOLVES to moonlight.
Begin SAD LOVE SONG.

Dietrich rises, places bucket upside-down beneath window,
stands on it, and gazes at full moon. He slowly removes
wire-rimmed glasses. Tear runs down his cheek. Our
attention is drawn from his eyes to full moon, which grows
larger.

INT. WINDOW - NIGHT

Pulling back, we see Maria gazing at moon through window.
Tear slowly runs down her cheek.

INT. CELL - NIGHT

We shift to see Hans lying flat on floor, hands folded
behind head, gazing at moon through window.

INT. WINDOW - NIGHT

Shifting, we see Christine gazing at moon through window.
Tear slowly runs down her cheek.

INT. BONHOEFFER PARLOR - NIGHT

We shift to see Dietrich's Mother gazing at moon through
window. Tears stream down her cheeks. Back to moon. SAD
LOVE SONG concludes. Loud CLANK! Ends scene.

INT. SOLITARY - DAY

Dietrich shocked awake by CLANK! He is thinner. Has two-
week beard. Knobloch stands at open door.

                    KNOBLOCH
          Prisoner Bonhoeffer, come with me.

Dietrich gets up stiffly and exits.

EXT. BONHOEFFER HOME - NIGHT

Address plaque, "Marienburger-Allee 43".

INT. BONHOEFFER PARLOR - NIGHT

Oster, Beck, Christine, Maria, and Dietrich's Mother
seated.

                    OSTER
          Frau Bonhoeffer, Christine, Maria ... we are
          sorry it has come to this.

                    CHRISTINE
               (concerned)
          Where are the files?!

                    BECK
               (gruffly)
          Don't worry! They're safe!

                    CHRISTINE
               (adamant)
          WHERE are the files?!

                    BECK
               (gruffly)

Per the contingency plan, they have been taken to
Colonel Schrader's hunting lodge!

                    CHRISTINE
          Are they all accounted for?!

                    OSTER
          Yes ... we believe so. We'll get word to Hans
          through the codes that they are safe.

Christine unsure. Maria and Dietrich's Mother worried.

                    BECK
          Those files document Nazi atrocities! They are
          nails in the Nazi coffin! Be assured we will
          guard them well!

                    MARIA
          They also implicate Dietrich and Hans.

                    BECK
          AND Oster, myself, Stauffenberg ... and many
          others!

                    DIETRICH'S MOTHER
          ... and Karl Barth, Bishop Bell ...

She breaks off and stares into space.

                    BECK
          I assure you! The files are SAFE!

Faces reflect uneasy hope that this is true.

INT. INTERROGATION ROOM - DAY

"April 29, 1943" fades in/out screen center. Dietrich sits
at large table opposite Roeder and others.

                    ROEDER
          Prisoner Bonhoeffer, you are aware of the charges
          against you?

                    DIETRICH
          No ... No, I am not. In fact, there was no
          warrant for my arrest.

Roeder smiles.

                    ROEDER
               (condescendingly)
          Prisoner Bonhoeffer. Did you really expect to
          avoid conscription under the guise of working for
          Counter-Intelligence?

Roeder LAUGHS. Dietrich flinches.

                    DIETRICH
          Dr. Roeder. Were my goal to avoid conscription,
          do you think I would have canceled my teaching
          appointment in America and returned to Germany?

Roeder flinches.

                    DIETRICH
          I am happy to serve my country through Counter-
          Intelligence ... and do so at the invitation of
          my brother-in-law, Hans von Dohnanyi, who seeks
          to use my ecumenical contacts.

Roeder twirls pencil in fingers and studies Dietrich. He
picks up document and continues...

                    ROEDER
          Superintendent Dibelius says that your church
          work has continued unabated. How is this
          possible when one is busy working for Counter-
          Intelligence?

                    DIETRICH
          Dr. Roeder, surely you can understand the
          necessity of preserving the fiction that my
          travels were primarily on church business.

Roeder shifts gears, hoping to catch Dietrich off guard.

                    ROEDER
               (quickly)
          Do you deny helping the Jew escape Germany in
          direct opposition to Our Leader's policy?!

Dietrich flinches.

INT. BORDER CHECKPOINT - NIGHT

Flashback to scene where Charlotte is handing papers to
Border Guard, who examines, then looks at her.

                    DIETRICH
          Dr. Roeder. I admit that I helped obtain the
          necessary papers for Fraulein Friedenthal to
          enter Switzerland. My understanding was that she
          was on assignment with Counter-Intelligence...

INT. INTERROGATION ROOM - DAY

Dietrich is responding to Roeder...

                    DIETRICH
          ... as are Communists, Poles...
               (raises his hand)
          ... Confessing Church pastors. Yes, I used my
          Swiss contacts to enable her to enter that
          country.

                    ROEDER
               (angrily)
          But this was AFTER the Reich specifically ordered
          that no Jew be allowed to leave the country!

Dietrich doesn't flinch.

                    DIETRICH
          I'm not sure of the exact date, Dr, Roeder. It
          certainly must have been prior to the State's
          order.

Roeder twirls his pencil calmly, then POUNDS the table and
SHOUTS...

                    ROEDER
          Prisoner Bonhoeffer! How do you account for the
          large number of Confessing Church pastors who
          serve in NON-combat military positions?!

EXT. BATTLEFIELD - DAY

Nazi soldiers thrown from force of EXPLOSION on
battlefield. Others take direct hit of bullets.

                    DIETRICH

                    (incensed)
          I resent the implication, Dr. Roeder. To the
          contrary, the record will show that not only have
          large numbers of our pastors served on the front
          lines, but a disproportionate number have given
          their lives for their country.

INT. INTERROGATION ROOM - DAY

Roeder waves him off and picks up document.

                    ROEDER
          I have, in your handwriting, a letter written to
          Hans von Dohnanyi...

Roeder looks up from document and studies Dietrich.

                    ROEDER
          ... requesting an appointment for one Wilhelm
          Niesel, a Confessing Church pastor, who, quote,
          "is *threatened* with conscription".

Roeder sets document down.

                    ROEDER
          Prisoner Bonhoeffer, what did you mean by
          THREATENED with conscription?

Dietrich flinches. We begin circling scene.

                    DIETRICH
          I will admit that, taken by itself, the word
          "threatened" does make a disagreeable impression.

Roeder watches Dietrich closely.

                    DIETRICH
          Yet, as I have just stated, the record is quite
          clear: one thing that can never be said of the
          Confessing Church is that we view military
          conscription as a threat.

Roeder twirls pencil and glares at Dietrich.

                    DIETRICH
          But, Dr. Roeder, you can certainly understand the
          anxiety of our pastors, who, despite their joy in

                    serving their nation on the front lines, remain
                    concerned about their churches back home.

Roeder SIGHS and rolls eyes.

                         DIETRICH
                    It is in this context that I sought to have
                    Pastor Niesel serve in a domestic non-combat role
                    while still pastoring his home church.

Roeder, disgusted, turns to confer with others, then spins
around to address Dietrich.

                         ROEDER
                         (roughly)
                    Prisoner Bonhoeffer, you are charged with
                    subversion of the military forces! You are to
                    obtain legal counsel and will be notified as to
                    the date of your trial.

Roeder readies to bang gavel.

                         DIETRICH
                    Might it be possible for me to have contact with
                    my family?

BANG! Roeder brings down gavel.

INT. PRISON CELL - NIGHT

Air raid SIRENS wail. Hans gathers papers in his cell.
Prisoners rush down hallway. Hans about to leave when
BOOM! His cell receives direct hit. Hans is crushed by
falling beams.

INT. SOLITARY - NIGHT

Dietrich in solitary. SIRENS. BOMBS heard in distance.
BOOM! Prison takes hit. SCREAMS. Lights out.

INT. SICKBAY - NIGHT

Prisoners crowded in sickbay. SIRENS, lights flicker,
periodic EXPLOSIONS. Dietrich dresses wounds of prisoners
on floor. Knobloch, Klinck, and Heinrich present. Schmidt
is curled up in corner, MOANING and CRYING.

                    KLINCK
               (sarcastically)
          So YOU'RE Bonhoeffer ... preacher and first-aid
          expert.

                    DIETRICH
          I do what I can.

Guard appears at doorway with more prisoners. Another bomb
EXPLODES. Knobloch SHOUTS...

                    KNOBLOCH
          No more room! Try next door!

All are tense.

                    HEINRICH
          We're going to die!

                    KLINCK
               (angrily)
          So why all this, preacher?!

SHOUTS in hallway. Lights out. CRIES. Lights back on.

                    DIETRICH
          Why not?

                    KLINCK
          What kind of answer is that?!

                    DIETRICH
          If there's no God, Klinck, why ask why? If no
          God, who is to say that what Hitler is doing is
          wrong?

                    HEINRICH
          No God ... no right, no wrong. Hitler says yes,
          you say no. Who's to say?

                    DIETRICH
          Exactly.

EXPLOSION. Building shakes. CRIES. Lights out, then on.

                    KLINCK
          Okay ... so where's God in all of this?!

Dietrich moves to attend to injuries of next prisoner,
clearly the Young Bearded Man.

                    DIETRICH
          Supporting those who are dropping bombs on us.

                    KLINCK
               (throws up his arms)
          Great! I don't support Hitler! So why are the
          bombs falling on me!

                    DIETRICH
          Because you live in Germany, 1943 ... among those
          who perpetrate evil. Do you expect God to have
          the bombs land only on the Nazis and not on the
          rest of us?

Dietrich moves to help next injured prisoner on floor.

                    KLINCK
          So God is powerless!

                    DIETRICH
          Not at all. He could kill every Nazi in a split
          second.

                    KLINCK
          So why doesn't he?

                    DIETRICH
          I'm not God. I do what I can ... and trust.

Transformer makes LOUD HUM. Schmidt HOWLS. Dietrich nods
toward him, cowered and CRYING in corner. Heinrich nods
toward Schmidt, and asks Dietrich...

                    HEINRICH
          So, what is it with Schmidt?

                    DIETRICH
          His mind is somewhere it doesn't belong.

                    KLINCK
          Okay, so whose fault is that?!

Another EXPLOSION. Lights flicker.

                         KNOBLOCH
          Hitler's.

They are surprised.

                         KLINCK
          Hey, who's side you on?

                         KNOBLOCH
          The bombs kill me as easy as they kill you. I
          have wife and little girl. I just do my job.

Dietrich gets up, walks toward Schmidt, kneels, and puts
his arm around him. All watch.

                         DIETRICH
          Partly Schmidt's fault, too. He's undoubtedly
          dwelt on the negative ... failed to trust.

Dietrich takes towel and wipes Schmidt's forehead.

                         DIETRICH
          And, Chance. He's probably wired differently
          than you, Klinck.

          HEINRICH
          And "Shut up, Schmidt" probably doesn't help.

                         KLINCK
                    (convicted)
          Probably not.

                         DIETRICH
                    (whispers)
          Hey, Schmidt. You want to talk?

Another EXPLOSION. Lights out.

INT. BONHOEFFER PARLOR - NIGHT

Christine in tears. She is comforted by Maria and
Dietrich's Mother. Beck and Oster offer condolences.

                         OSTER

It was a direct hit. Hans has a brain embolism.
His speech and vision are blurred ... and he is
partially paralyzed.

                    BECK
               (gruffly)
          Does he have his wits about him?!

                    OSTER
               (perturbed)
          He's in no conditioned to be interrogated, if
          that's what you mean!

Maria looks up.

                    MARIA
          And Dietrich?

                    OSTER
          Unhurt ... as far as we know. His hearing
          concluded with a charge of subversion. He is
          awaiting trial.

                    BECK
               (gruffly)
          Hans' trial must come first!

                    OSTER
          But Hans' HEARING hasn't concluded. He hasn't
          been charged ... and he is in no condition...

                    BECK
               (cuts him off)
          Can't be helped! This was all agreed to
          beforehand!

                    MARIA
          You mean Dietrich has to just sit there!

                    OSTER
          I'm sorry, Maria. Hans has an exceptional legal
          mind. We can't risk Dietrich bearing the brunt
          of Gestapo questions about Counter-Intelligence.

                    BECK
          Hans' trial MUST come first!

                    OSTER
          We'll get word to Dietrich through the codes. He
          can receive parcels every Wednesday now.

                    DIETRICH'S MOTHER
          Encourage him to put his mind on his studies. It
          will help pass the time.

                    OSTER
          Maybe this nightmare will be over soon.
          Gersdorff is ready for another attempt.

The women look at each other.

EXT. WOODEN FIELD OFFICE - NIGHT

Floodlights illuminate scene. Hitler exits limo along with
cronies, walks around vehicle, through cordon of stiff-
saluting officers, and into Wooden Field Office.

We turn 180 degrees to see Gersdorff lugging heavy knapsack
up steep hill immediately adjacent to Wooden Barracks,
across from Field Office. He trips. The sack hits the
ground. He pops up and examines contents. Bomb
accidentally triggered. He fiddles with it to no avail,
looks around, tosses it underneath barracks, and hustles to
top of hill next to barracks entry. NAZI OFFICER and
Immoral Woman walk down sidewalk, drunk and LAUGHING. They
turn and begin to go up steps into barracks. Gersdorff
grabs Nazi Officer's arm, tries to pull him away, shaking
his head "No". Nazi Officer puts foot on Gersdorff's chest
and shoves him away. Gersdorff tumbles backward onto the
ground.

                    NAZI OFFICER
          A moralist, huh? Listen, little man, I will do
          what I want to do! Got it!

Nazi Officer and Immoral Woman LAUGH and proceed into
barracks. Gersdorff's eyes bulge. He turns, runs from
building, diving for cover into the dark. Barracks BLOWS
SKY HIGH!

INT. PRISON CELLS - NIGHT

SIRENS blare, bombs EXPLODE, lights flicker, prisoners rush
down corridor.

INT. SICKBAY - NIGHT

Prisoners packed in sickbay. SIRENS wail. Lights swinging
and flickering. Dietrich and medic tend to injured.
Schmidt follows Dietrich, staying close wherever he goes.
All are quiet, some standing, some sitting, all watching
Dietrich.

                    KNOBLOCH
          Every night, same thing.

                    KLINCK
          Then help us get out of here.

                    KNOBLOCH
          Yah, you go free and my wife and little girl lose
          Papa. I don't think so.

                    HEINRICH
          Cool it, Klinck. Think about someone other than
          yourself for once.

EXPLOSION. Lights flicker. Klinck looks disgustedly at
Schmidt, who is close to Dietrich's side.

                    KLINCK
               (angrily)
          So God lets Schmidt go crazy, lets Hitler rise to
          power, and lets the bombs fall on us. Some God!

Heinrich rolls eyes.

                    DIETRICH
          He's given humans free will. Schmidt chose not
          to trust. A plurality voted for Hitler. The
          Nazis are evil.

                    KLINCK
               (angrily)
          So God is responsible for evil!

All look at Dietrich.

                    DIETRICH
          Not at all. He wants us to love. Love is
          impossible absent free will. If you want love,

you must have the possibility not to love, which
can lead to evil. If you give your son an auto,
and he uses it to purposely run someone over,
does that make you guilty of murder? Of course,
not.

Bomb BLAST. Lights off, then on. Dietrich moves to attend
another injured person. Another EXPLOSION. Transformer
HUMS, SPARKS, and dies. Lights out. All are quiet.

EXT. STREET SCENE - NIGHT

Christine, Oster, and Beck illuminated by lamplight. They
glance about. Beck agitated, as is Christine.

                    BECK
          What do you want?! This is dangerous!

                    CHRISTINE
          General Beck! Hans' wants those files destroyed!

                    BECK
          Destroyed?! I already told you, we can't do
          that! Those files are needed to prosecute the
          Nazis!

                    OSTER
          You assured him they were safe?

                    CHRISTINE
          He said, "I don't care about history! Tell them
          this will cost heads! The files implicate us
          all! They must be destroyed!"

                    BECK
          Tell Hans it won't be much longer! But they will
          remain where they are!

                    CHRISTINE
          Are you sure they are safe?!

Beck throws up his hands in frustration. Oster intervenes.

                    OSTER
          Christine. We are right on the verge! The
          Allies are advancing ... but we are not waiting.

EXT. TARMAC - DAY

Holding thick briefcase, Stauffenberg exits small plane,
enters passenger's side of waiting military limousine, and
speeds away.

                    OSTER
          Colonel Stauffenberg is making another attempt on
          Hitler tomorrow.

INT./EXT. AUTOMOBILE - DAY

Forested area. Stauffenberg rides in speeding limo. "July
20, 1944" fades in/out screen center.

                    BECK
          He has direct access to Hitler now! Reports to
          him three times a week on the status of
          replacement soldiers needed for the front!

EXT. WOLF'S LAIR - DAY

Nazi compound encircled by tall metal fencing topped with
barbed wire. Limousine pulls up and Stauffenberg exits
with briefcase. Chauffeur leaves to park auto.

                    BECK
          Once we confirm that Hitler is dead, we
          commandeer the radio station, secure Berlin, and
          announce an interim government! Hans will be
          free!

Stauffenberg glances around, squats, opens briefcase, lifts
papers, flips back cloth, uses tweezers to crush vial of
acid inside bomb, flings tweezers into underbrush, resets
items, and closes briefcase.

                    OSTER
          He only has ten minutes after he trips the fuse.

Stauffenberg trots up to first checkpoint, manned by Bruno.
Stauffenberg shows ID, but holds onto briefcase.

                    STAUFFENBERG
          I'm late, Bruno. Make it quick.

                    BRUNO

I check everything. Leave early next time.

                    STAUFFENBERG
               (handing him briefcase)
          My report today is not good. More replacements
          are needed at the front. Shall I tell Hitler
          that you volunteer?

Bruno stops short of opening case, and hands it back to
Stauffenberg.

                    BRUNO
          Funny man. Leave early next time.

Bruno opens gate. Stauffenberg hurries down path to second
checkpoint, which grants entry to Main Building. Schmitz
guards gate.

                    STAUFFENBERG
          Running late, Schmitz. Let me through.

                    SCHMITZ
          Have to check ID.

Stauffenberg hands him ID.

                    SCHMITZ
          Need to check the briefcase ... regulations.

                    STAUFFENBERG
               (handing him briefcase)
          You're going to make me late, Schmitz.

Schmitz opens briefcase. Papers on top. Brandt pokes his
head out of door.

                    BRANDT
          Stauffenberg. There you are. You're next.
          Forget it, Schmitz.

Schmitz looks at Brandt, then at Stauffenberg.
Stauffenberg eyes Schmitz, who slowly closes briefcase,
hands it to Stauffenberg, and opens gate. Stauffenberg
hustles to door and says to Brandt...

                    STAUFFENBERG
          Unbelievable headwind.

Brandt slaps Stauffenberg on back. Startled, Stauffenberg
steadies briefcase.

                    BRANDT
          Hey, kid. I said you would succeed, didn't I?
          This is the big time!

                    STAUFFENBERG
          Yes sir. I hope you are right.

Brandt looks puzzled. Stauffenberg notices. Their eyes
lock momentarily.

INT. HALLWAY - DAY

Stauffenberg and Brandt walk past desk manned by another
Guard. Stauffenberg speaks to Guard.

                    STAUFFENBERG
          I'm expecting an urgent call from Berlin. Let me
          know when it comes.

Begin GRADUALLY INCREASING RUSHING SOUND. Brandt opens
door and walks in. Stauffenberg stops, takes deep breath,
and follows.

INT. WAR ROOM - DAY

Sawhorses at either end support heavy oaken planks, forming
an 18' x 5' table covered with maps. Hitler is seated in
middle on long side, with back to door. Directly across
table, a General is reporting (silent to us). Brandt takes
seat. Fifteen others sit around table.

Hitler acknowledges Stauffenberg. General uses pointer to
emphasize location on map. Hitler turns attention to map,
takes magnifying glass, rises, and leans over table to
inspect location being discussed. Several others do so as
well.

Stauffenberg approaches table, feigns interest in map, then
carefully places briefcase under table and pushes it toward
Hitler with foot. He then backs unnoticed towards door.
Brandt changes position for closer look and hits foot on
Stauffenberg's briefcase. Stauffenberg freezes. Hitler
looks back at Brandt, who looks under table, picks up

briefcase, sets it under far end of table, and returns to
map. RUSHING SOUND at its LOUDEST.

INT. HALLWAY - DAY

Stauffenberg rushes past Guard at desk. RUSHING SOUND
begins RECEDING GRADUALLY. Stauffenberg barely audible.

                    STAUFFENBERG
          Forgot something in the auto. Hold my call.

Guard rises ... but Stauffenberg is gone.

EXT. WOLF'S LAIR - DAY

Stauffenberg hurries to first gate.

                    STAUFFENBERG
          Forgot something in the auto.

Puzzled Schmitz opens gate. Stauffenberg hustles through.
He eyes Schmitz, then glances toward building.

INT. WAR ROOM - DAY

Hitler turns to look for Stauffenberg, then looks at
Brandt, who looks toward briefcase, then locks eyes with
Hitler.

EXT. WOLF'S LAIR - DAY

MASSIVE EXPLOSION. Schmitz horrified. Stauffenberg turns
and hustles toward second gate.

Badly injured Brandt stumbles from partially demolished
building and SHOUTS...

                    BRANDT
          Secure all exits! No one gets out!

Panicked, Schmitz turns to see Stauffenberg running up rise
toward second gate. He grabs telephone and SHOUTS.

                    SCHMITZ
          Bruno! No one exits! No one exits!

                    STAUFFENBERG

>   (mutters to himself)
>   Bruno!

Stauffenberg hustles over rise and up to second gate. He
stops short, shocked. General GABE is talking with Bruno,
who is wholly focused on attention being given him by a
General and is oblivious to Schmitz' SHOUTS coming through
receiver in left hand. Faintest glint of light sparks from
one of Gabe's eyes. He points at button.

>   GABE
>   And what does this do?

>   BRUNO
>   (presses button)
>   That's how I open the gate.

Gate opens. Stauffenberg hesitates, then hustles through
open gate ... unnoticed.

>   GABE
>   Ah, technology. How do you stay on top of it
>   all?

>   BRUNO
>   Some can, some can't. It's part of my job,
>   General.

Stauffenberg runs down path toward parking lot.

>   GABE
>   I must commend you to Hitler.

Bruno, suddenly aware of Schmitz' SHOUTS, presses phone to
ear.

>   BRUNO
>   (shouts)
>   Explosion?! What explo...?

MASSIVE BOOM! SHOCK WAVE moves through second gate. Bruno
aghast! He grabs second phone and SHOUTS...

>   BRUNO
>   Block the road! Block the road! No one escapes!
>   No one esc...

Dumfounded, he draws pistol and begins chasing after
Stauffenberg, BLASTING AWAY! At parking lot, Stauffenberg
SHOUTS to chauffeur, who stands next to auto, gawking at
the rising smoke...

                    STAUFFENBERG
          Quick! We need to get help!

As Stauffenberg jumps into passenger seat, Gabe suddenly
steps in front of chauffeur.

                    GABE
          I've got it.

Chauffeur notices stripes on Gabe's sleeve, clicks heels,
and gives stiff-arm salute. Gabe hops into driver's seat
and PEELS OUT as Bruno and contingent of Storm troopers
send HAIL OF BULLETS toward auto, which speeds away in
cloud of dust.

INT./EXT. AUTOMOBILE - DAY

Gabe speeds around corner, encounters Storm trooper
vehicles set as roadblock. Stauffenberg ducks below
dashboard as HAIL OF BULLETS penetrates windshield. He
glances up just as bullet RIPS into Gabe's hat, sending it
flying. Gabe swerves off road, flies up over rise, vehicle
in air, lands backwards, does 180 on ground, GUNS IT back
onto road and around bend. Stauffenberg stares wide-eyed
at Gabe, who checks rear view mirror and smiles. He looks
at Stauffenberg.

                    STAUFFENBERG
          Who...?

                    GABE
          Tell the pilot to start down the runway!

Stauffenberg rises partially, grabs military phone, and
dials. Storm troopers give chase in several vehicles from
rear, leaning out of windows and FIRING weapons.

                    STAUFFENBERG
                 (to pilot)
          Go! Go! Fly over us! Drop the rope!

Auto swerves onto and then down runway. Small plane comes
up low from behind, rope dangling from open door. Plane is
just above auto. Stauffenberg SHOUTS to Gabe...

                    STAUFFENBERG
          What about you?!

                    GABE
          Don't worry about me! Go to Stockholm, NOT
          Berlin! You'll have enough fuel.

Faintest glint of light sparks from one of Gabe's eyes.
Stauffenberg puzzled. Trooper vehicles swerve onto runway
in pursuit. Guns BLAZING. Knotted rope hits window.
Stauffenberg reaches out, grabs several knots up with good
hand, glances at Gabe, maneuvers body half-way out side
window, and tugs at rope. Stauffenberg pulled out, dangles
beneath slowly rising plane, locks both feet on bottom
knot, climbs knots with one good hand and feet. Bullet
RIPS through shirt collar, BLASTING OFF colonel insignia.
Another RIPS through rope, severing cords. Rope is pulled
into plane, which slowly rises into sky.

Aerial view as Storm trooper vehicles surround Gabe's auto,
which has come to a stop on runway amidst a HAIL OF
BULLETS. Troopers exit vehicles and throw open door. Auto
is empty.

INT. SMALL PLANE - DAY

Stauffenberg, breathing heavily, plops into co-pilot's
seat.

                    STAUFFENBERG
          He said "Go to Stockholm, not Berlin".

                    PILOT
          Who said?

                    STAUFFENBERG
          I ... I'm not sure.

Pilot give Stauffenberg puzzled look.

                    PILOT

Not enough fuel for that. Hitler's dead! Our
orders are to go to Berlin and help secure the
city.

                    STAUFFENBERG
          I know. I know.
               (pause) (quietly)
          He said we'd make it.

They both glance at fuel gage.

                    PILOT
          Where to, Colonel?

We focus on Stauffenberg.

                                        DISSOLVE TO:

INT. BONHOEFFER PARLOR - NIGHT

Dietrich's Mother, Christine, and Maria are huddled around
radio, listening, worried.

                    ANNOUNCER
          ... repeat: four officers were killed and twelve
          others wounded as a bomb exploded inside the East
          Prussian Headquarters of Our Leader. Reich
          Security reports that the bomb was delivered by
          Colonel Claus von Stauffenberg, who has since
          been captured. The next voice you hear will be
          that of Our Leader.

Women near tears.

                    HITLER
          My German comrades! I am unhurt, aside from
          minor bruises and burns ... confirmation once
          again that my course of action is blessed by
          Divine Providence.

Women shake heads.

                    HITLER
          ... Have no fear. I will crush and destroy the
          criminals who have dared to oppose themselves to
          Providence ... and to ME!

Women CRY.

INT. PRISON CELLS - NIGHT

Dietrich opens parcel containing stack of books. He runs
his finger over author on title page of book one. Sets it
aside. Book two. Author's name is underlined. He flips
to last page, then five pages forward. A "B" is lightly
underlined in pencil. Dietrich writes "B" on slip of
paper. Five pages forward. An "E" lightly underlined.
Dietrich writes "E". Five more pages. "C" lightly
underlined. He writes "C". SIRENS begin to wail.
Prisoners YELL. Knobloch comes down hall, unlocking
doors...

                    KNOBLOCH
          Line up! End of hall! I'll be there to
          unlock...

BOOM! Cells take direct hit. SCREAMS. Many injured.
Dietrich struggles from cell. Debris everywhere. He digs
rubble off Klinck. Heinrich does same for Schmidt.
Schmidt and Klinck lie near each other. The wall between
their cells is gone. Knobloch draws pistol and SHOUTS.

                    KNOBLOCH
          Everyone stay where you are!

Knobloch stands guard. MOANS come from injured. He nods
toward Dietrich, who quickly removes his shirt, rips it
into a tourniquet, and ties it on Klinck's bleeding leg.
Heinrich rips off shirt and places it under Klinck's head.
Schmidt mangled. Dietrich cradles his head in arms.
Schmidt looks at him and says weakly...

                    SCHMIDT
          Thank you, Jesus.

Schmidt dies. Dietrich choked up. Klinck YELLS. Still
holding Schmidt, Dietrich reaches over to Klinck, who
splutters...

                    KLINCK
          Pray for me, Bonhoeffer!

                    DIETRICH
                 (tenderly)

                    Pray for yourself, Klinck.

                         KLINCK
                         (weakly)
                    Jesus ... I'm sorry. Forgive me...

Klinck dies. Dietrich puts other arm around Klinck's head
and hugs him. In choked voice, he says softly...

                         DIETRICH
                    He did, Klinck. He did.

We slowly pull back from scene, stop, and then begin slow
zoom onto scrap of paper on floor, which reads, "BECK
SUIC".

INT. OFFICE - DAY

Roeder at desk. "September 22, 1944" fades in/out screen
center. Stack of files on left, another on right. He
reads. Suddenly...

                         ROEDER
                    Ha! And there it is!

He smiles, CHUCKLES, and closes file.

INT. PRISON HOSPITAL ROOM - DAY

Bars on windows. Hans lies on bed, emaciated. Roeder
walks in and flips file onto bed.

                         ROEDER
                    Take a look! Evidence we've been seeking for two
                    years!

Hans, in great pain, turns on side, opens file, looks, then
reclines again and closes eyes. Roeder LAUGHS.

                         ROEDER
                    Plans for a coup in Oster's handwriting. Beck's
                    notes of conversations, contact with the Brits
                    ... It's all there, Dohnanyi.

                         HANS
                         (slurred)
                    Where did you find this?

Roeder picks up file.

                    ROEDER
          In the former offices of Counter-Intelligence.

                    HANS
              (startled, slurred)
          I don't believe you.

Roeder SNAPS file under shoulder.

                    ROEDER
          Believe it!
              (taunts)
          We won't execute you just yet. First we want to
          tickle your toenails to learn just who was in on
          these plots!

Roeder motions to orderlies.

                    ROEDER
          Bring the prisoner!

EXT. COUNTRY ROAD - NIGHT

Headlights from parked autos partially illuminate Knobloch,
Maria, and Dietrich's Father. "October, 1944" fades in/out
screen center. Maria helps Knobloch put packages into
auto.

                    DIETRICH'S FATHER
          Change of clothes, food, ration cards, cash.
          We'll hide you, your family, and Dietrich outside
          Berlin until the war is over.

All set. Knobloch looks around nervously.

                    MARIA
          You're a brave man and a good friend, Knobloch.

She kisses him on cheek.

                    KNOBLOCH
          I risk it for family ... and for Bonhoeffer.
          Gestapo will not kill Bonhoeffer. He is good
          man.

Knobloch gets into auto and drives into the night.

INT. INTERROGATION ROOM - DAY

Dietrich sits at large table opposite Roeder and others.

> ROEDER
> Prisoner Bonhoeffer! As you may know, Hans von
> Dohnanyi is in custody ... as is Colonel Oster
> and several others. And I am sorry to report
> that fate has claimed Colonel Stauffenberg and
> General Beck.

Dietrich stares at him.

> ROEDER
> A rather sordid business for a pastor to get
> into, wouldn't you say?
> (gruffly)
> Our Leader wants names Bonhoeffer! A confession
> ... and names!
> (evilly)
> Do you value your toenails?

Dietrich flinches.

> ROEDER
> Or how about your parents? Or ... what's her
> name? Maria?

Dietrich looks at Roeder in anger. Roeder LAUGHS.

INT. SOLITARY - NIGHT

Dietrich sits on floor, hands and feet shackled, head back
against wall.

EXT. BEACH - DAY

FLASHBACK to scene where Six-Year-Old Dietrich whispers
into Dietrich's Young Mother's ear.

INT. SOLITARY - NIGHT

Observation hole opens. Knobloch whispers.

                    KNOBLOCH
          Bonhoeffer!
               (pause)
          It's all set!

Dietrich stares up at light coming through tiny window.

EXT. BONHOEFFER GARDEN - NIGHT

FLASHBACK to scene where Dietrich and Maria gaze into each
others eyes in moonlit garden.

INT. SOLITARY - NIGHT

Dietrich sighs.

                    DIETRICH
          I can't do it.

                    KNOBLOCH
          What?! You'll be tortured and killed!

Tear rolls down Dietrich's cheek.

EXT. BONHOEFFER HOME - NIGHT

Address plaque, "Marienburger-Allee 43", dangles from
damaged brick pillar. Noise of BATTLE in distance.

INT. BONHOEFFER KITCHEN - NIGHT

Kitchen damaged. Christine, Maria, Dietrich's Father, and
Dietrich's Mother seated at table.

                    CHRISTINE
          Hans says they've discovered everything ...
          absolutely everything!
               (chokes up)
          They are being tortured.

Dietrich's Father puts arm around Mother, who wipes away
tear with tissue. Maria is numb.

                    CHRISTINE
               (almost in whisper)
          He says he would rather die than see those faces
          again.

Christine clears her throat.

                    CHRISTINE
          Hans wants his next parcel to have diphtheria
          blended into the jam.

Maria closes her eyes.

                    CHRISTINE
          He says if he is seriously ill, the interrogation
          may be delayed. He doesn't want to unwittingly
          implicate the others while being tortured.

                    DIETRICH'S FATHER
          I'll get some from the lab.

EXT. PRISON - DAY

Winter storm. "February 7, 1945" fades in/out screen
center. Dietrich and others being crammed into prison van.
GUARD hands papers to Driver.

                    GUARD
          Buchenwald.

INT. BONHOEFFER PARLOR - DAY

Parlor damaged. Dietrich's Mother opens door. Maria
stumbles in from cold, exhausted, parcel in arms.
Dietrich's Father and Mother hurriedly tend to her.
Dietrich's Mother takes parcel and sets it on table.

                    MARIA
          I couldn't deliver it. They've moved Dietrich!
          I don't know where he is!

Dietrich's Mother looks worriedly at Dietrich's Father.

                    DIETRICH'S FATHER
          Probably a camp to the south. We're being
          squeezed by Soviets on the east and British and
          Americans on the west.

Maria startled.

                    MARIA

                    (mutters)
          Extermination camp!

She jumps up.

                    MARIA
          I must find him. Pack warm clothes and food for
          Dietrich. I must find him.

Dietrich's parents are concerned for Maria.

INT./EXT.   TRAIN - DUSK

Maria, clutching parcel, is reflected in broken window of
moving train. She stares at neighboring highway crowded
with Refugees, walking, pulling wagons. Snowing heavily.
Smoke in air. BOMBS in distance.

                    PASSENGER A
          Refugees. It seems the whole of Germany is here.

                    PASSENGER B
          Where will we find food? And petrol?

EXT. TRAIN STATION - DUSK

Maria exits train. Sign reads, "WEIDEN". Snowing heavily.
Passengers A and B begin to walk away.

                    MARIA
          Excuse me. Which way to Flossenburg?

Passengers A and B look at each other.

                    PASSENGER B
          Down that road, Fraulein, into the valley. But
          it's twelve miles.

                    MARIA
          Thank you.

Maria starts walking. Passengers A and B shake their
heads.

EXT. ROAD - DUSK

Maria jostled as she walks against flow of refugees carrying their belongings. REFUGEE grabs her by arm.

                    REFUGEE
          You're going the wrong way, Fraulein. The
          Soviets are coming.

Maria tightens grip on parcel and keeps walking. Noise of BATTLE in hills. Black smoke amid heavy snow.

EXT. IRON GATE - NIGHT

Maria, exhausted, stumbles up to iron gate. Sign on gate reads, "FLOSSENBURG". She turns and leans with her back against it, then rolls and stumbles toward small guardhouse adjacent. GATE GUARD sticks head out. Overhead light illumines scene.

                    GATE GUARD
          Yes, Fraulein?

                    MARIA
          Bonhoeffer. I have a parcel for Dietrich
          Bonhoeffer.

Guard reaches for clipboard. He flips through names.

                    GATE GUARD
          No Bonhoeffer, Fraulein. Not here.

He retreats into guardhouse and closes door. Maria left in cold. She claws her way along gate, sinks to her knees, and SOBS.

                    MARIA
          Dietrich! My Dietrich!

EXT. CONCENTRATION CAMP - DUSK

Raining. Wood-burning truck is parked at entrance. "April 5, 1945" fades in/out screen center. Dietrich and others, including Young Bearded Man, loaded into enclosed rear of truck. They position themselves around wood. Door is closed and locked. Truck rumbles away.

INT. HITLER'S OFFICE - DAY

Hitler extremely agitated. His cheeks are flushed with
rage. His body is trembling as he shakes his fist in every
face.

                    HITLER
          If the German people are to be defeated, they
          have been too WEEK! They have failed to prove
          their mettle before HISTORY!

He pushes Storm trooper back on heels.

                    HITLER
                 (screams)
          Leave nothing to the enemy! I said, NOTHING!

He whirls on another Trooper.

                    HITLER
          Scorch the earth! Destroy it all! Leave them
          NOTHING!

He whirls and points at Himmler.

                    HITLER
          And execute everyone connected with the
          conspiracy! They must not survive! Do you
          hear?! THEY MUST NOT SURVIVE!!

INT. BACK OF WOOD-BURNING TRUCK - DAY

Dark. Raining outside. Prisoners sit around wood, some
with backs against sides of truck, which jostles down
highway.

EXT. SMALL TOWN - DAY

Wood-burning truck stops next to sign reading, "WEIDEN".
Raining heavily.

INT./EXT. BACK OF WOOD-BURNING TRUCK - DAY

Prisoners listen to VOICE in rain.

                    VOICE
          Drive on, we can't take you ... too full!

Truck rumbles off. DISSOLVE to sound of SIRENS and
motorcycles closing in on truck. Truck slows and stops.
Rear door opened. Light partially reveals prisoners.

                    OFFICER
          Prisoner Schneider! Prisoner Liedig!

OFFICER leans over to Partner and points to name on list.

                    OFFICER
          Starts with a "B" ... can't make it out.

Two prisoners exit truck. Then a third, the Young Bearded
Man, hops out. Dietrich drops back into shadows. Officer
looks at third prisoner, closes door and SHOUTS...

                    OFFICER
          Okay! You can go!

Dietrich's eyes closed. His head bounces against side of
truck as it rumbles away. DISSOLVE to LOUD BANG! Truck
swerves right and left. Prisoners tumble. Truck stops.

                    PRISONER A
          Broken steering.

Rain DRUMS on roof.

EXT. ROADSIDE - DAY

Small bus with unbroken windows pulls up. Prisoners are
transferred to bus. Still raining.

INT./EXT. BUS - DAY

. Semi-luxury. Prisoners feeling good. Bus pulls away.
Broken-down, wood-burning truck fades into distance.
DISSOLVE to bus turning left and beginning climb into
mountains. Clouds dissipate. Sun comes out. CUT to bus
pulling up in front of school building. Small mountain
town.

EXT. SCHOOL BUILDING - LATE AFTERNOON

Prisoners get off bus and are taken up wooden stairs into
first floor of school building.

INT.   SCHOOLROOM - LATE AFTERNOON

Room pleasantly decorated. Beds, linens, curtains. Guard
locks door. Prisoners look at each other and CHEER.

                    PRISONER A
          Do you believe this?!

They LAUGH. Some flop on mattresses. Some do high-fives.
Dietrich goes to window and sits on chair in ray of warm
late afternoon sunlight. He removed wire-rimmed glasses.
Prisoner A walks up to same window and looks out.

                    PRISONER A
               (mutters)
          Come on ... Yanks!

Dietrich looks at him and smiles.

INT.   PRISON WARD - NIGHT

Dark. BANG! Door opens. Storm trooper with lantern
barges in. Prisoners MOAN as they are awakened. Trooper's
light reveals prisoners lying on floor. He shines light
into the face of PRISONER B and SHOUTS...

                    STORM TROOPER
          YOU are Bonhoeffer!

                    PRISONER B
          No! I am not!

He shines light into face of PRISONER C.

                    STORM TROOPER
          YOU are Bonhoeffer!

                    PRISONER C
          No! I am NOT Bonhoeffer!

INT.   SCHOOLROOM - DAY

Beautiful bright morning. "April 8, 1945" fades in/out
screen center. Prisoners share bowl of boiled potatoes and
loaf of bread.

                    PRISONER A

Pastor Bonhoeffer. It's Sunday. Lead us in
worship, won't you?

                    DIETRICH
          Well, I...

                         PRISONER A
          Please. We are thankful ... and I think we may
          soon have even more to be thankful about.

Prisoners encourage Dietrich. He consents. DISSOLVE to
Dietrich standing and speaking. He faces door opposite.

                         DIETRICH
          The first Sunday after Easter. Resurrection.
          New life. Isaiah says, "All we like sheep have
          gone astray. We have turned every one to his own
          way. And the Lord has laid on HIM the iniquity
          of us all."

We pan the prisoners.

                         DIETRICH
          "Surely he has borne OUR griefs and carried OUR
          sorrows. He was pierced for OUR transgressions
          and bruised for OUR iniquities..."

Sunlight streams from window. Prisoners at peace.

                         DIETRICH
          "...the chastisement of OUR peace was upon HIM.
          And with HIS stripes, WE are healed."

We focus on Dietrich.

                         DIETRICH
          "Yet he shall see the light of life, for he bore
          the sins of many ... and by him many shall be
          justified."

                                        DISSOLVE TO:

                         DIETRICH
          Jesus said, "I am the resurrection and the life.
          Whosoever believes in me, though he were dead,
          yet shall he live ... and whosoever lives and
          believes in me ... shall never die."

Prisoners bask in words. Brief pause, then cloud disperses
sunlight and cold chill blows in. Door suddenly swings
open with a BANG!

                    STORM TROOPER
          Prisoner Bonhoeffer, come with us!

It begins raining. Begin REPRISE of "GIVE ME JESUS".
Dietrich calm. He walks toward door, hands Bible to
Prisoner A and whispers...

                    DIETRICH
          This is the end ... but for me, it is the
          beginning of life!

Prisoner A choked up. Others stunned. Dietrich exits,
followed by Storm trooper.

EXT. SCHOOL BUILDING - DAY

Dietrich bounds down stairs into waiting van. Troopers
enter. Van speeds away. Prisoners watch from window.

EXT. IRON GATE - NIGHT

Van moves through open iron gate with sign that reads,
"FLOSSENBURG".

INT. ROOM - NIGHT

Dimly lit room. Roeder sits at small table. Dietrich
brought in, shackled hand and foot. Oster and a few other
prisoners are already there. Dietrich's and Oster's eyes
catch. DISSOLVE to Roeder BANGING gavel angrily and
SHOUTING (silent to us). He motions to Storm troopers.
Prisoners escorted out.

INT. PRISON CELL - EARLY MORNING

SLAM! Guards swing door open. They have stretcher.
Startled Hans is lifted onto it and carried out.

EXT. PRISON - EARLY MORNING

Guards flip stretcher. Hans lands crumpled onto the
ground. He looks up. Storm trooper FIRES machine-gun in
his direction.

INT. PRISON CELL - EARLY MORNING

Open door reveals Dietrich on knees in prayer. "April 9,
1945" fades in/out screen center. Silent SHOUT of Guard
begins SLOW MOTION. Dietrich calmly looks at Guard and
rises. Guard SHOUTS again (silent to us). Dietrich begins
removing prison top.

EXT. STONE WALKWAY - EARLY MORNING

Above-waist view of Dietrich, Oster, and others prisoners
walking down stone stairway, beneath trees, toward
execution site.

EXT. EXECUTION SITE - EARLY MORNING

Smoke rises from smoldering pile of burning bodies. Meat
hooks spaced five feet apart hang from concrete wall.
Piano wire hangs from each hook. Wooden stairs lead up to
scaffold underneath hooks. Guards stand at ground level in
front of scaffold. Above-waist view as prisoners walk up
wooden stairs, Dietrich last. We move into the head of
Dietrich and view the next sequence from his eyes.

Young Bearded Man walks into execution site from side
opposite scaffold. His eyes are on the prisoners. Guard
walks down scaffolding, lifting piano wire around each
neck. Wire placed around Dietrich's (our) neck. Dietrich
reaches up with shackled hands and removes wire-rimmed
glasses (view now blurred), and hands them to Guard.

                    DIETRICH
              For my mother, please.

Guard SLAPS glasses from Dietrich's hand and crushes them
underfoot. He CLAMORS down stairs. Oster cries out.

                    OSTER
              Bonhoeffer!

                    DIETRICH
              Think of Jesus, Oster! Think of Jesus!

                    GUARD
          Ready ... pull!

End SLOW MOTION. Our out-of-focus view suddenly drops
three feet. END REPRISE of "GIVE ME JESUS" and blend into
REPRISE of MOVIE THEME.

Young Bearded Man, now in focus, is dressed in white.
Guards go about their business in background. We come out
of Dietrich's head and see him standing in white. Dietrich
looks into twinkling eyes of smiling Young Bearded Man.

                    DIETRICH
          My Lord!

                    YOUNG BEARDED MAN
          Well done, Dietrich!

They LAUGH. Young Bearded Man puts right hand on
Dietrich's shoulder and nods to his left. There is Oster,
dressed in white. He LAUGHS and walks up to Dietrich and
Young Bearded Man. The three embrace.

EXT. FIELD - DAY

The three come out of embrace amid extremely vivid colors
on a little rise in green field. Blue sky. Majestic
mountains in distance. Young Bearded Man's eyes twinkle as
he steps aside to reveal scene.

Thousands of people--black, red, yellow, white--are dressed
in a variety of white outfits, particular to their
activity. Dietrich hears his name being called.

                    HANS
          Dietrich!

He spins around to see Hans, dressed in white, grinning
from ear to ear. They LAUGH and slap each other on the
back. Young Bearded Man LAUGHS. Hans nods to left to
reveal Dietrich's Young Mother, dressed in white, who gives
Dietrich a big hug, after which he looks at Young Bearded
Man and says...

                    DIETRICH
          How...?

                    YOUNG BEARDED MAN
             There's no time here, Dietrich.

They all look at each other and LAUGH. Dietrich's Young
Mother looks to her right. Standing there are Christine,
Gerhard, Sabine, Frank, and Franz. All in white and
LAUGHING. Young Bearded Man walks up to Dietrich and turns
him around. There stands Maria, beautiful in white.

                       DIETRICH
                     (in whisper)
                Maria!

They run into each other's arms for a long embrace.

We pull back slowly and see the multitudes engaged in
various activities. Young Bearded Man walks down rise,
picks up errant football, motions to Ernie, a young black
man.

                    YOUNG BEARDED MAN
                Go deep, Ernie.

Ernie heads out for long pass. Young Bearded Man throws
and connects. We continue to pull back. Credits roll. At
END of MOVIE THEME REPRISE, begin REPRISE of UPBEAT SONG
(orchestral version) until credits end.

A Note about Characters and Events

By necessity historical screenplays cannot recreate every event or include every person involved in those events. Life is more complicated than a screenplay. Accordingly, *Bonhoeffer: A Screenplay*, includes only those events essential to the flow of the story, and some, like the scene of Dietrich and Maria in the garden, have been fabricated to add depth. Likewise, so not to overwhelm the viewer with characters, some, like Barth, Himmler, Oster, and others, play their own part and others as well. And again to add depth, some characters like Heinrich, Klinck, and Schmidt have been fabricated. Similarly, although much of the dialogue has an historical base, it most always has been edited into bytes that the viewer can absorb. Accordingly, to assist the reader in putting this screenplay into its historical context, the following details the actual chronology of events in the life of Dietrich Bonhoeffer.

Main Screenplay Characters

DIETRICH, Dietrich Bonhoeffer (1906-1945), one of eight children born into the affluent family of Karl and Paula Bonhoeffer, is raised in Berlin where his father is a renowned professor of psychiatry and his mother a descendent of eminent theologians. He receives a doctorate in theology at age twenty-one from the University of Berlin, despite favoring the neo-orthodoxy of Karl Barth at the University of Gottingen, who holds to the possibility of revelation, rather than the liberalism of the Berlin faculty, who do not.

While on a fellowship at Union Theological Seminary in New York, Dietrich is introduced to a church in Harlem by fellow student, Frank Fisher. The stark contrast between theology as an intellectual pursuit, as practiced at Berlin and Union, and the Christian faith as a practical reality in the lives of people makes a lasting impression on Dietrich, such that he considers himself not to have been a Christian prior to this point.

Upon his return to Germany, Dietrich vocally opposes Hitler's infiltration of the German church, speaks publicly on the radio against Hitler's growing influence (which address is cut short), rallies pastors to officially protest Hitler's efforts, helps found the Confessing Church in opposition to the Reich church (the former German church), trains pastors at the newly-formed Confessing Church seminary, assails the Gestapo for harassing the Confessing Church, and rallies ecumenical opposition to the Reich church. Dietrich encourages Barth to pen the Barmen Declaration, which represents a line in the sand verses the Reich church, after which Barth is summarily ousted from Germany. Dietrich is forced to train pastors underground when the Nazis eventually board up the Confessing Church seminary doors.

Hitler's continued harassment of the Confessing Church—disrupting its services, confiscating its funds, sending its pastors to the war front and others to concentration camps—effectively silences the movement. Confused, Dietrich returns to Union in New York as he is about to be conscripted into the armed forces; however, once there, he is conscience-stricken and immediately returns to Germany to join the Resistance in its efforts to remove Hitler from power. His military call-up is deferred as brother-in-law, Hans von Dohnanyi, arranges for him to work for Counter-Intelligence, where he actually becomes a double-agent, working to subvert the Nazis through his ecumenical contacts. He is eventually arrested and imprisoned, along with Dohnanyi and other members of the Resistance, and has a positive influence in the lives of his fellow-prisoners. He also corresponds regularly with his eventual biographer, Eberhard Bethge.

Shortly after the failed July 20, 1944 assassination attempt on Hitler, secret files hidden by Dohnanyi to be used in documenting Nazi atrocities are discovered, and all connected with the conspiracy are marked for death. Dietrich is executed on April 9, 1945, less than a month before the surrender of Germany and the end of the war in Europe.

Dietrich leaves behind several writings, three of which have become classics: *Life Together*, a treatise on the church; *The Cost of Discipleship*, which argues against cheap grace; and *Letters and Papers from Prison*, which contains the seeds of his thoughts about religionless Christianity.

BARTH, Karl Barth (1886-1968), Swiss professor of theology at the Universities of Gottingen, Muster, and Bonn, and after his ouster from Germany, at the University of Basel. Founder of neo-orthodoxy, which in opposition to liberal theology holds to the possibility of revelation. Barth authors the Barmen Declaration (personally mailing a copy to Adolf Hitler), which exposes the Reich church as no church at all and gives birth to the Confessing Church. Although initially questioning Dietrich's involvement as a double-agent, Barth later supports Dietrich's efforts. Screenplay economy is taken to have Barth be the one Dietrich encourages to contact England on behalf of the Resistance (actually it was the ecumenist Willem Visser 't Hooft) and to have Barth meet the escaping Charlotte Friedenthal at the Swiss border.

BECK, Ludwig Beck (1880-1944), German Military Chief of Staff, is later head of the Resistance and is its designated provisional head-of-state should Hitler be ousted in a military coup. Beck opposes Hitler's rush to war, tries to organize generals against it, and subsequently resigns his post, thereafter joining and leading the Resistance, not for moral reasons, but solely to prevent Germany's military defeat. Deeply involved in several failed attempts on Hitler's life, Beck commits suicide after the attempt on July 20, 1944 and the discovery of his involvement.

BRANDT, Heinz Brandt (1907-1944), Lieutenant-Colonel on Hitler's General Staff, unknowingly carries the bomb that fails to detonate aboard Hitler's plane, and inadvertently saves Hitler's life by moving the bomb-laden briefcase prior to its detonation on July 20, 1944. Brandt dies from injuries one day later.

CHRISTINE, Christine von Dohnanyi, sister to Dietrich and wife of Hans von Dohnanyi, is actively involved in the Resistance, arrested and imprisoned, but subsequently released. Screenplay economy precludes the inclusion of Dietrich's brother, Klaus, an attorney, who is also an active member of the

Resistance, as were his sister, Ursula, and her husband, Rudiger Schleicher. Like Dietrich and Hans, Klaus and Rudiger are executed by the Nazis.

FRANK, Frank Fisher, Union Theological Seminary student from Alabama, introduces Dietrich to the Harlem church, which proves instrumental in Dietrich's transition from theologian to Christian. Screenplay economy is taken to have Frank travel to Mexico with Dietrich (it was actually fellow Union student, Jean Lasserre of France) and to have Frank be the catalyst in Dietrich's decision to return to Germany (actually it was Dietrich's choice alone).

FRANZ, Franz Hildebrandt (1909-1985), Jewish Christian student of Dietrich at the University of Berlin and later activist pastor along with him in opposing Hitler's efforts to seize control of the German church, is forced to flee Germany following his arrest and release for opposing the Nazis. He subsequently serves a church in Cambridge, England, teaches at an American university, and concludes his ministry as a pastor in Scotland.

GABE, Gabriel, one of two archangels (the other is Michael) mentioned in the Jewish and Christian scriptures as spirit beings through whom God speaks and executes judgment on rare occasions.

GERHARD, Gerhard Leibholz (1901-1982), Jewish Christian husband to Dietrich's twin sister, Sabine, escapes to England with his wife and daughters just as Hitler begins to persecute the Jewish people. He and his family return to Germany after the war, where, as an attorney, he becomes a leading figure in establishing the constitutional rule of law in the new Germany.

GERSDORFF, Rudolf von Gersdorff (1905-1980), German military officer and member of the Resistance, fails in his attempt to sacrifice his own life while simultaneously taking Hitler's as the latter's entourage exits the building far ahead of schedule. Editorial liberty is taken to make Gersdorff's physical stature that of fellow conspirator, Helmuth Stieff.

GOERING, Hermann Goering (1896-1946), Commander-in-Chief of the German Air Force and selected by Hitler to be second-in-command within the Nazi hierarchy. Convicted and sentenced to death at the Nuremburg Trials, Goering commits suicide the night prior to his scheduled execution.

HANS, Hans von Dohnanyi (1902-1945), husband to Dietrich's sister, Christine, an attorney heavily involved in the Resistance, is strategically positioned within the Reich Ministry of Justice and subsequently the German Military Intelligence Office, a hotbed of the Resistance that was always suspected by the Gestapo. Hans meticulously documents Nazi atrocities for eventual use in prosecuting the perpetrators, but the secret file's contents, upon discovery, seals the doom of the conspirators, including Dietrich. Hans is executed by the Nazis.

HEINRICH, KLINCK, and SCHMIDT are fictional characters through whom the viewer gains a sense of the positive impact that Dietrich has upon his fellow-prisoners, the latter, Schmidt, representing an actual prisoner who wailed all the time. KNOBLOCH is the actual name of the prison guard who is so moved by Dietrich's character that he becomes involved in a plot to help him escape, which escape is called off by Dietrich at the last minute for fear of repercussions that would fall upon his parents and Maria. BRUNO is likewise a fictional character representative of the Storm Troopers.

HIMMLER, Heinrich Himmler (1900-1945), Head of the Gestapo, overseer of concentration camps, extermination camps, and killing squads, is the most feared man in Nazi Germany next to Adolf Hitler. Himmler is directly responsible for the deaths of over six million Jewish people, and perhaps another three million Polish citizens and others deemed unworthy of life by the Nazis. He commits suicide just prior to the Nuremburg Trials.

HITLER, Adolf Hitler (1889-1945), native Austrian and founder of National Socialism, rises to the position of German Chancellor via the plurality democratic vote of the people, immediately establishes a dictatorship, ruthlessly eliminates all opposition, exterminates millions of people in concentration and extermination camps, and initiates World War II, which spreads death and destruction across the continent. Hitler survives several attempts on his life, orders the execution of those connected with the plots, including Dietrich, and eventually takes his own life when he realizes the Nazi effort has failed.

MARIA, Maria von Wedemeyer (1924-1977), eighteen years Dietrich's junior and one-time confirmation student of his, subsequently re-enters Dietrich's life and becomes engaged to him just prior to his imprisonment. Maria eventually settles in the United States, marries, and works in the computer industry as a mathematician.

MULLER, Ludwig Muller (1883-1945), anti-Semite, pro-Nazi pastor selected to be Head Bishop of the Reich church. Muller commits suicide after the Nazi's are defeated.

OSTER, Hans Oster (1887-1945), German Army general, a leading member of the Resistance, is second-in-command to fellow-conspirator Wilhelm Canaris at Counter-Intelligence. Screenplay economy dictates that the characters of Oster and Canaris be combined, and that Oster stand in for Henning von Tresckow in the failed attempt to detonate a bomb aboard Hitler's plane. Oster and Canaris are executed along with Dietrich at the Flossenburg extermination camp the morning of April 9, 1945.

ROEDER, Manfred Roeder, Nazi Prosecutor, arrests and interrogates Dietrich and Hans, charging them with subversion of the armed forces. Screenplay liberty is taken to have Roeder and Bruno be the face of the Gestapo in harassing the Confessing Church, and to have Roeder be the one who confronts Hans with the secret files and who eventually condemns Dietrich to death. Nazi Prosecutor Walter Huppenkothen actually confronts Hans and sentences Dietrich.

SABINE, Sabine Leibholz, sister to Dietrich and wife of Gerhard Leibholz, flees Germany with Gerhard and daughters, Marianne and Christiane, as Hitler closes the border to the Jewish people, which includes Gerhard.

STAUFFENBERG, Claus von Stauffenberg (1907-1944), a leader in the Resistance, strategically positioned as a Lieutenant-Colonel on Hitler's General Staff, delivers the July 20, 1944 bomb that comes closest to killing Hitler. The failure of this attempt results in the collapse of the Resistance, the identification of its members, and their subsequent execution, including Dietrich's. Screenplay economy also has Stauffenberg involved in the ill-fated attempt to place a bomb aboard Hitler's plane, which bomb-laden package is actually delivered and subsequently recovered by Fabian von Schlabrendorff. Stauffenberg is executed by the Nazis.

YOUNG BEARDED MAN, eternally-existing outside of time, enters the material realm in human form as the son of Mary of Nazareth, subsequently bearing for all human beings the full wrath of God upon the sin of mankind in his suffering and execution by the Romans in AD 30, thereby enabling all who turn to God in repentance to be forgiven of their sins and restored to a right relationship with him, rises from death and returns to the spiritual realm, from which he cares for all who live a life of faith, i.e., acting on their belief in him as their Savior from sin and seeking to live a life of love, i.e., being what he has asked us to be and doing what he has asked us to do. The screenplay erases the popular notion of him as being unknowing, uncaring, and irrelevant in modern life, and likewise erases the notion of him as a bumbling softie who forgives everybody for everything. He is seen as being aware of every detail, of being present but unseen at every happening, as being present during our worship, of crying at the evil perpetrated by human beings, of being the one served as we serve others, of largely allowing the God-ordained operators of cause-effect, chance, and human choice to run their course, but, on occasion, intervening directly in human affairs. He is seen as the ultimate judge of human beings, who welcomes into his eternal kingdom those whose faith on earth gave indication of their being in right relationship with him. He is also seen not as some stiff, effeminate, untouchable holy man, but as one who takes joy in heaving a football. He is the star of the screenplay.

Bonhoeffer: A Chronology

German Political Background

Established in 1871, the German Empire united free cities, independent states, duchies, principalities, and kingdoms, plus Alsace-Lorraine, land ceded by France at the conclusion of the Franco-German War. Chancellor Otto von Bismarck turned this new nation into an industrial giant that took pride in its military strength and prowess. Distaining parliamentary government, Bismarck concentrated power in the executive branch. He also isolated old-enemy France from Russia by developing the Triple Alliance with Italy and Austria-Hungary, the latter of which included many German-speaking peoples. In response to the Triple Alliance, France and Russia forged an agreement that became the Triple Entente when joined in 1907 by Britain, the latter being concerned over German expansion under Kaiser Wilhelm II following his dismissal of Bismarck.

The tempest that led to World War I began when Austria-Hungary laid claim to Bosnia and Herzegovina, and Germany demanded compensation for land claimed by France in Morocco. War was averted when France gave Germany the French Congo knowing, however, that it was infested with sleeping sickness. Italy's seizure of Tripoli in 1911 encouraged the Balkan States to initiate hostilities against Turkish rule in an effort to gain independence. When Austrian Archduke Ferdinand was killed by a Serbian terrorist in June 1914, Austria-Hungary issued an ultimatum to Serbia, causing the Serbs to mobilize their forces, leading Austria-Hungary to declare war on Serbia, at which Russia mobilized its forces against Austria-Hungary, causing Germany to issue an ultimatum to Russia, at which France mobilized against Germany, leading Germany to declare war on France, Great Britain to declare war on Germany, and Austria-Hungary to declare war on Great Britain. WWI was under way.

The Life of Dietrich Bonhoeffer

1906

Dietrich is born February 4 in Breslau, the largest city in Silesia, a state in Prussia, part of the Imperial German Empire. His ancestry is traced to Schwäbisch Hall, a district in south-central Germany, where his forebears were goldsmith émigrés from Holland. His father, Karl, is a Professor of Psychiatry and Neurology, the son and grandson of eminent theologians. His mother, Paula von Hase, descends from eminent jurists. With twin sister, Sabine, Dietrich has older brothers Karl-Friedrich, Walter, and Klaus, sisters Ursula and Christine, and will have a younger sister, Susanne. Walter will be killed in World War I and Klaus will be executed in the conspiracy together with the husbands of Ursula (Rüdiger Schleicher) and Christine (Hans von Dohanyi). Sabine will emigrate to England prior to World War II with her Jewish Christian husband, Gerhard Leibholz.

1912

The Bonhoeffer family moves to Berlin as father Karl takes a post in psychiatry there. Bonhoeffer neighbors include liberal theologian Adolf von Harnack, historian Hans Delbruck, and physicist Max Planck. Here the dragonfly incident with mother and 6-year-old Dietrich occurs. The large family, requiring a governess, nursemaid, chambermaid, housemaid, and cook, settles on an acre garden in a spacious home with many rooms, including a school room with desks (mother teaches each child at home for one or two years), a girls room with dolls, a boys work room with carpenter bench, and an animal room replete with squirrels, snakes, lizards, butterflies, beetles, and birds.

1913

Seven-year-old Dietrich starts school at the Friedrichs-Werder Gymnasium, fearful of having to cross a long bridge between there and home. He is also afraid of water, having to be taken out of the swimming line, although he later becomes an excellent swimmer. The family is active together, reading plays aloud, producing them, and holding recitals, with Dietrich providing accompaniment on the piano at age 8. His father encourages intellectual rigor and clear thinking and expression, cautioning "never to use a hollow phrase".

1914-1918

During World War I, the Bonhoeffers open their home to a refugee family from the East and to a cousin who had been blinded in battle. Dietrich and Sabine hold long conversations about death and eternity, Dietrich falling silent on occasion at gatherings, only to be found later deep in thought. At night in bed, he would tap "think of God" in code on the wall separating him from his twin sister's room,

At the Gruenwald Gymnasium, where among other subjects he now studies Greek, Hebrew, and Latin, 11-year-old Dietrich responds to the master's question by stating that he wishes to study theology, which elicits stares and snickers from his classmates. In response to brother Klaus' chide that the church is a boring, feeble institution, Dietrich replies, "Then I shall reform it," and in answer to brother Karl-Friedrich's efforts to dissuade him, young Dietrich states, "You may knock my block off, but I shall still believe in God."

Karl-Friedrich, 19, is wounded and Walter, 18, is killed in battle, events which devastate Dietrich's mother. Dietrich is given Walter's Bible as a confirmation present three years later and begins serious personal Bible study at this time. He uses Walter's Bible the rest of his life.

1918
Political upheaval follows the German Navy's mutiny in Keil. Bavaria claims independence. Kaiser Wilhelm flees to Holland. German Communists Karl Liebknecht and Rosa Luxemburg proclaim a German Soviet regime from the steps of the Imperial Palace, while Paul Scheideman and the Social Democrats are proclaiming a German Republic from a window of the Reichstag Building. A November 11 armistice ends WWI.

1919
A bloody attempted coup by the German Communists fails. The Treaty of Versailles is signed on May 19, creating despair, resentment, and a sense of injustice throughout Germany. The Treaty places full responsibility for WWI on Germany, requires enormous reparations, the surrender of all colonial possessions, the return of Alsace-Lorraine and the Saar Basin coal fields to France, surrender of the Polish Corridor to Poland (separating East Prussia from rest of Germany), establishes Danzig as a free city, and imposes a drastic reduction on the German army. Germany enters five years of economic chaos. The democratic Weimar Republic is established on August 11.

1923
A Paris meeting of WWI Allies declares Germany in default on reparation payments, at which France and Belgium occupy the Ruhr. Germany retaliates by halting all production of coal and steel in the region, which sends its own tottering economy into a tailspin. Inflation takes off, bankrupting large sections of the populace. Inflation, unemployment, and resentment rouse German nationalism. Klaus writes prophetically to fellow law student Hans von Dohnanyi regarding obnoxious National Socialist (Nazi) classmates, "These are the people we shall have to do with later."

Following a family tradition, 17-year-old Dietrich enrolls at the University of Tubingen, where his father attended. He studies theology and lives with sister Christine, who is studying biology, and his grandmother, Julie Bonhoeffer. He joins the *Hedgehogs*, a social group to which his father belonged, but ceremoniously resigns when they refuse to protest against Nazi demands.

Adolf Hitler steps into the political spotlight during his trial for treason following a failed National Socialist coup in Munich. The trial gives wide coverage to Nazi views. Sentenced to five years in prison, he gains release after six months and resumes leadership of the National Socialists. Germany experiences an economic upturn following Chancellor Gustav Stresemann's successful negotiation with the Allies to reduce the annual reparation payments and to loan money to Germany. Recovery is aided by the evacuation of the Ruhr by France and Belgium.

1924
Dietrich, 18, and Klaus, 23, tour Rome and northern Africa. Dietrich is impressed by the multinational nature of the church as he encounters throngs at St. Peter's and monks with white, black, and yellow faces. He transfers to the University of Berlin to continue his study of theology and lives at home. The Berlin faculty, led by Harnack, view theology as historically developed, whereas the Gottingen faculty, led by Karl Barth, view it as revelation. In this battle between Christian culture (Harnack) and passion for the central truth itself (Barth), Dietrich learns thoroughly from Barth's opponents while siding with Barth.

Social Democrats take 27% of the Reichstag seats, Catholic Centre 14%, Communists 9%, and National Socialists 3%.

1925-1927
In addition to his studies, Dietrich teaches a children's class on Sundays, takes them on outings, and holds discussions at his home. At age 21, he defends his dissertation, *The Communion of Saints*, which develops the idea of the church as Christ in community. He befriends Franz Hildebrandt, a young Jewish student and later co-worker.

1928
Dietrich, 22, leaves for Barcelona, Spain, where he serves a one-year vicarage required for ordination. The congregation doubles in size as Dietrich emphasizes the Christian faith as a living reality. He starts a children's service, a discussion group for boys, and an organization to help with unemployment and vagrancy.

1929
Dietrich begins a required internship for professors at the University of Berlin, writing his thesis *Act & Being*, in which he argues against philosophy being pressed into the service of theology, since philosophy is man's attempt to arrive at truth through via his own thought and is thereby self-centered. The Christian faith, Dietrich writes, is a matter of God's revelation in Christ. Man doesn't go to God; he comes to us.

The German economy succumbs to worldwide depression. Two-and-one-half million Germans are out of work. Germany defaults on reparation payments. Anger rekindled vis-à-vis the Treaty of Versailles is exploited by the Nazis on the Right and the Communists on the Left. Josef Goebbels becomes the Nazi Minister of Propaganda.

1930

Catholic Centre's Heinrich Bruning is appointed Chancellor and initiates economic retrenchment in a vain attempt to meet German reparation commitments. The Communists and Nazis whip up anti-Weimar sentiment. As unemployment jumps to 3 million, the Nazis suddenly gain 22% of the Reichstag seats, compared with 25% for the Social Democrats and 16% for the Communists.

Dietrich's thesis is accepted by the University, after which he immediately begins a yearlong sabbatical at Union Theological Seminary in New York. Regarding Union, Dietrich comments, "A theology is not to be found here ... They chatter till all is blue without any factual foundation ... They intoxicate themselves with liberal and humanistic expressions, laugh at fundamentalists, and basically they are not even a match for them... Often it goes through and through me when here in a lecture they dismiss Christ, and laugh outright when a word of Luther's is quoted on the forgiveness of sins." And with respect to the typical New York church, he says, "One may hear sermons in New York upon almost any subject; one only is never handled, or at any rate so rarely that I never succeeded in hearing it presented: namely, the gospel of Jesus Christ, of the cross and forgiveness, of death and life... But what do we find in the place of the Christian message? An ethical and social idealism which pins its faith to progress, and which for some not quite evident reason assumes the right to call itself Christian. And in the place of the Church as a community of believing Christians stands the Church as a social institution. Anyone who has seen the weekly program of one of the large New York churches, with its daily, almost hourly events, tea parties, lectures, concerts, charitable events, sports, games, bowling, dancing for people of all ages..."

Frank Fisher, a Black student, introduces Dietrich to life in Harlem, where he makes many friends, leads a Sunday school class, a women's Bible study, and a Vacation Bible School, visits the residents in their homes, and gets to know them well. Jean Lassere, a French student at Union, interests Dietrich in the Ecumenical Movement (although Dietrich is skeptical of the Movement's weak theology) and to pacifism (although Dietrich never becomes a thoroughgoing pacifist).

1931

Dietrich and Lassere head to Mexico for the summer in an ancient Oldsmobile, camping along the way. When the auto breaks down, they travel by train, eventually limping back to New York in the patched-up Olds. Back in Germany, Dietrich meets Karl Barth for the first time; however, they apparently talk past each. Dietrich attends a meeting of the ecumenical World Alliance in Cambridge and is elected to office following his argument that the Alliance must establish itself on a sound theological basis. Dietrich teaches at the University of Berlin, attracting many students to his lectures. Ordained into the ministry in November, he teaches a confirmation class of 50 boys in the rough Wedding district of Berlin.

Internal dissension mounts within the German Church as the "German Christians" (pastors supporting Hitler) argue that God's will is for them to unite behind a strong ruler and keep the Aryan race untainted. German unemployment reaches 4.35 million.

1932

Dietrich takes up residence in the Wedding district, devotes more time to the boys and their families, and invites them home for supper, games, chess, outings, Bible study, and catechism. He loves it, stating, "I can hardly tear myself away from it." He chastises the German church in his Reformation Day sermon at Kaiser Friedrich Memorial Church, comparing the German church to the First Century church at Ephesus, which had "lost its first love", saying, "Our Protestant church has reached the eleventh hour of her life. We have not much longer before it will be decided whether she is done for or whether a new day will dawn. It is high time we realized this ... faith and repentance mean letting God be God and to be obedient to him in our actions, especially in our actions." Regarding the Bible: "One cannot simply read the Bible like other books. One must be prepared really to inquire of it. Only thus will it reveal itself ... because it is in the Bible that God speaks to us... If it is I who determine where God is to be found, then I shall always find a God who corresponds to me in some way, who is obliging, who is connected with my own nature. But God determines where he is to be found ... and I have since learned to read the Bible in this way... I had already preached often, I had already seen a great deal of the Church and talked and preached about it ... but I had not yet become a Christian."

Paul von Hindenburg is re-elected President of Germany in a runoff vote, garnering 53% of the total. Hitler finishes second at 37%. Hindenburg appoints not Hitler, but Franz von Papen as Chancellor, at which storm troopers go on a rampage, killing over a hundred and wounding many more. In July Reichstag elections, National Socialists take a whopping 38%, compared to 22% for the Social Democrats and 15% for the Communists. Parliamentary gridlock ensues, resulting in a call for November elections, which gives the Nazis 34% of the seats, Social Democrats 21%, and Communists 17%. Hindenburg replaces von Papen with Kurt von Schleicher; however, he too is unable to form a government. Unemployment in Germany reaches 6.1 million by year's end (one of every three workers).

1933

To get the government moving, Hindenburg agrees to appoint Hitler as Chancellor, banking on von Papen as Vice Chancellor, the Social Democrats, and the Catholic Centre to keep him and the National Socialists in check. Hitler immediately dissolves the Reichstag and calls for March elections. The day following Hitler's January 31 appointment, Dietrich's radio address on "The Concept of Leadership" is abruptly cut off.

Arson heavily damages the Reichstag Building in February. Blaming the Communists, Hitler initiates Emergency Measures "for the present" that restrict free speech, the press, the privacy of letters, telegrams, and telephone calls, and broadens powers for conducting searches of houses and personal property. Hitler arrests hundreds, bans Communist and Social Democratic publication (rendering them unable to combat Nazi propaganda during the upcoming election), and gives free reign to the storm troopers, who proceed to terrorize political opponents. National Socialists take 45% of the Reichstag seats, Social Democrats 19%, and Communists 13% in this, the final German political election until the end of WWII. Within four months, all political parties other than the National Socialists are banned. Defying the Treaty of Versailles, Hitler calls for arms-equality with other major powers, begins rearmament, refuses to pay reparations, advocates incorporation of all German-speaking peoples within the Third Reich, encourages National Socialist parties in other nations, forms alliances with Japan and Italy, calls for the destruction of democratic Czechoslovakia, and awards jobs to those supportive of National Socialism. The German economy begins to recover, causing Hitler to be viewed by many as a hero who rescued the Fatherland from malaise, chaos, and humiliation, while resurrecting national pride and creating jobs.

Mindful of the disproportionate number of Jewish persons active within the Communist party, Hitler calls for an April 1 boycott of all Jewish-owned shops. Here occurs the screenplay's episode with Dietrich's grandmother, Julie Bonhoeffer. Hitler adds the "Aryan Paragraph" to the Civil Service Code, which eliminates all government workers of Jewish descent.

The "German Christians" attempt to establish a National Reich Church at a meeting in Eisenach. They nominate Ludwig Muller for Bishop, but the vote goes to a moderate, Friedrich Bodelschwingh. Enraged, the "German Christians" refuse to recognize the new National Reich Church, take over the

Church in Prussia, and install Joachim Hossenfelder as head, a man who referred to the "German Christians" as "Storm Troopers for Jesus Christ". The Young Reformers (pastors opposed to the Nazi infiltration of the church) prove ineffectual due to their adherence to Luther's doctrine of the separate spheres of church and State. Dietrich and Franz consider starting a Free Church (separate from the government), but discard the idea. Dietrich protests against applying the Aryan Paragraph to church workers, stating that membership in the Church can never be based on race. Nonetheless, a referendum of German churches gives overwhelming support to the "German Christians".

The Vatican signs the Concordat, agreeing not to interfere in German political matters as long as the Nazis leave the Catholic Church alone.

Karl Barth issues a call to action, upon which Dietrich and Herman Sasse author the Bethel Confession on behalf of the Young Reformers. However, after its circulation for comment among twenty theologians, it is reduced to a shell, which even Dietrich refuses to sign. The "German Christians", fully in control of the National Reich Church, move to adopt the Aryan Paragraph at their "Brown Synod" (brown is the Nazi color) in September and to install sympathetic bishops throughout Germany. In response, the "Emergency League of Pastors" is established by the Young Reformers led by Martin Niemoller, Gerhard Jacobi, Dietrich, and Franz. The Emergency League immediately calls for a mass resignation of pastors, allegiance to the scriptures and Confessions alone, repudiation of the Aryan Paragraph, united resistance to any attack upon them, and the provision of material and financial support for those suffering from repressive laws. The Emergency League gains the signatures of 2,022 pastors.

Dietrich attends the September World Alliance meeting in Sofia, Bulgaria, and leads the effort "to deplore German state measures against the Jews, especially considering them as inferior, and to protest the German Church's adoption of the Aryan Paragraph." Dietrich and Franz fail in their effort to prevent Ludwig Muller from being elected as National Bishop. Muller is enthroned in a spectacular coronation replete with Nazi trimmings. Frustrated, Dietrich takes a pastorate in Sydenham, London—drawing a rebuke from Barth—where he becomes the leader of German pastors in England and develops a valuable friendship with Anglican Bishop George Bell, a leader in the World Alliance and a member of the British House of Lords. Dietrich keeps Bell informed on developments in Germany.

The "German Christians" commit a major blunder at a November Rally in the Sports Palace, where 20,000 swastika-wearing attendees gather amidst Nazi banners, placards, the march of storm troopers, and the music of Nazi brass bands. Berlin Nazi Party Leader Reinhard Krause rails against the Old Testament and "Rabbi Paul," telling his audience to accept from the gospels only that which "speaks to the German heart" which, he says, "is entirely consistent with the demands of National Socialism." A massive outcry ensues, causing Hitler to resolve to undermine the church rather than work through it.

1934

Hitler prohibits comments opposing Reich Church policy in public, by leaflet, or any other means, upon threat of removal from pastoral office. Dietrich telegrams the Reich Church office requesting clarification as to whether this prohibition applies to German pastors in England. The English contingent proceeds to publicly state their lack of confidence in Bishop Muller and their desire to align with the Pastor's Emergency League.

Hitler pulls a ruse on the Emergency League at a meeting arranged ostensibly to forge peace, but where Goering rushes in on cue to tell those gathered of an intercepted telephone call in which Niemoller had bragged of Hindenburg's influence over Hitler and had threatened to establish a Free church if matters were not resolved to the satisfaction of the Emergency League. Hitler feigns injury at Niemoller's comments and requests all present to assure him of their loyalty, citing "this momentous occasion" when the rift can be settled in the very presence of the Chancellor. An emboldened Muller sets forth new regulations and suspends all opposition pastors, including Niemoller.

Reich Church envoy Theodor Heckel travels to England to meet with German pastors, making clear that opposition to the National Bishop is opposition to the State (treason). He can manage only one signature of loyalty to the Bishop. Heckel likewise fails to win support in a meeting with Anglican Bishop Bell, warning him not to interfere with German affairs. After returning to Germany, Heckel summons Dietrich to appear before him on German soil. Dietrich obliges and is presented with a document to sign, stating that he will abstain from all ecumenical activities not authorized from Berlin and that his failure to do so would be regarded as "involvement with foreign intervention into the internal affairs of Germany." Dietrich asks for time to consider, returns to England, and writes to Heckel that he cannot and will not sign the document.

After Dietrich tells Bell that nothing less than Christianity on the Continent is at stake, Bell issues his Ascensiontide Letter to churches throughout the world, stating: "A revolution has taken place in Germany ... the chief cause of anxiety being the assumption by the Reich Bishop of autocratic powers ... without precedent in the history of the Church ... the exercise of which are incompatible with the guidance of the Holy Spirit." Karl Barth authors the Barmen Declaration, six statements regarding the nature of the true church in Germany, including: "Jesus Christ, as He is testified to us in Holy Scripture, is the one Word of God which we have to hear, and which we have to trust and obey in life and death. We reject the notion that the church would have as the source of its proclamation still other powers, figures, and truths." This Declaration gives rise to the "Confessing Church", immediate recognition of which is sought of the World Alliance by Dietrich, claiming that it only is the true Protestant Church in Germany. Dietrich seeks invitation to the Confessing Church as the official German representative at the Alliance's upcoming meeting in Fano, Denmark, which effort is strongly protested by the Reich Church. Dietrich's request is denied. Bell, however, secures an invitation for a single "advisory" representative of the Confessing Church.

Hitler initiates a purge of Communists, Jewish people, and political opposition, even dissidents within the Nazi Party. On June 30, Ernst Rohm, Kurt von Schleicher, and 70 suspected Nazi party members are executed. Feigning innocence, Hitler orders the execution of the executioners. At this point, the *London Times* prints the statement that is read on the BBC in the screenplay. Hitler declares himself both Chancellor and President following the July death of Hindenburg, thus seizing absolute control. He prefers the title, "The Leader". The Nazis bring every sector of Germany under central control: industry, commerce, agriculture, science, education, and religion. All social, trade union, and cultural activities and institutions are now under the umbrella of National Socialism.

Although the tireless efforts of Dietrich and Bishop Bell win Fano World Alliance delegate support of the Confessing Church over the Reich Church, Heckel manages to have an amendment passed that grants the Reich Church a permanent invitation to all future World Alliance meetings. Hitler imprisons Bavarian and Wurtemberg bishops in for failing to actively support the Reich Church. The Confessing Church is officially established at its October conference in Dahlem, and requests that Dietrich train pastors at its fledgling seminary in Finkenwalde, just east of Stettin in Pomerania. He accepts and develops a friendship with student Eberhard Bethge, his eventual biographer.

1935
The World Alliance meeting in Chamby, Switzerland, takes no position on the German situation. The presence of Heckel and the Reich Church delegation causes the Confessing Church to forego attending based upon its stance that the Reich Church has absolutely nothing to do with the Church of Jesus Christ. The Reich Church creates dissension among Confessing

Church pastors by inviting them to participate on Committees convened ostensibly to find avenues of compromise between the Reich Church and the Confessing Church. Dietrich states, "between Church and pseudo-Church there can be no cooperation."

The Nazis remove Barth from his position at the University of Bonn for failing to pledge loyalty to Hitler, an oath now required of all university professors. Barth takes a position at Switzerland's University of Basel. To get after Finkenwalde, Hitler initiates the "Fifth Emergency Measure of the National Church" forbidding "unauthorized" churches from ordaining or appointing pastors, forming policy, dispersing funds, holding meetings, or operating seminaries. Finkenwalde is illegal.

1936

Dietrich persists with training at Finkenwalde, giving each student his blessing should they choose to leave in light of the Fifth Emergency Measure. All stay. At Dietrich's February 4 birthday party, the students ask him to show them this larger church of which he continually speaks, whereupon he secures invitations from churches in Denmark and Sweden for his students to visit as their guests. Upon their return, the Reich strips Dietrich of his right to lecture at the University of Berlin, to which he replies, "I have long ceased to believe in the university." The Reich increases harassment of Finkenwalde graduates, imprisoning Johannes Pecina, a pastor in Seelow, imprisoning his replacement, Willi Brandenburg, but leaving his replacement, Adolf Pruess alone. The episode causes the Finkenwalde students to consider their own futures.

The Confessing Church begins to unravel. As a counterpart to the Reich Church Committees, the Confessing Church sets up its own Committees for determining what is necessary for German church unity. Pastors must now choose which effort to support. When many choose to participate on the Reich Church Committees, Dietrich writes, "The boundaries of the Church are the boundaries of salvation. He who separates himself from the Confessing Church separates himself from salvation," which statement is widely condemned.

In June, Prussian Confessing Church pastors send a memo to Hitler criticizing the Reich's treatment of Jewish people and the oppressive measures being used against the Church. After Hitler ignores the memo, Finkenwalde students Werner Koch and Ernst Tillich leak it to a newspaper. The Gestapo demands identification of the leakers, causing debate that further splits the Confessing Church. After discovering Koch and Tillich, the Gestapo sends them and Jewish Christian Friedrich Weisler to the

Sachsenhausen concentration camp. Weisler is tortured and beaten to death. From this point forward, a Finkenwalde graduate is always in prison.

1937

Abandoning its charade of Church Committees, the Reich Church begins outright suppression via rigorous enforcement of the Fifth Emergency Measure. Confessing Church collections are seized, sermons monitored, and pastors arrested. Dietrich tries to convince the World Alliance of the serious nature of the situation, but only Bell understands. The Alliance continues to recognize the validity of the Reich Church. Dietrich concludes that ecumenical efforts have failed.

Arrests for violating the Fifth Emergency Measure intensify during the summer. Only July 1, Dietrich and Bethge arrive to discuss the crisis at Niemoller's home, only to be met by Franz, who informs them that Niemoller had just been arrested by the secret police. When Franz catches sight of a black Mercedes pulling up outside, the three try to escape through the back door, only to be met by a Gestapo official and herded back into the sitting room. After seven hours of house arrest and meticulous searching, the Gestapo discovers and confiscates 30,000 marks, the entire treasury of the Pastor's Emergency League. Niemoller is taken to Sachsenhausen.

As families arrive for worship at Franz' church on August 8, they find the building cordoned off by police. When the crowd refuses to disperse, all are arrested, including Franz. Dietrich's father secures Franz' release, whereupon he is sent to England for the duration. Finkenwalde doors are sealed by the Gestapo in September. Dietrich begins *The Cost of Discipleship*, which is now a classic on what it means to be a follower of Jesus.

At a secret November 5 meeting, Hitler informs the German military leadership of his intent to satisfy Germany's territorial demands by force. Army Chief Werner von Fritsch objects and is dismissed. Hitler assumes Supreme Military Command early the following year. Behind the scenes, Chief of Staff General Ludwig Beck (eventual leader of Resistance) tries to raise his fellow generals in revolt.

1938

Hitler upbraids Austrian Chancellor Kurt von Schuschnigg for cracking down on National Socialists in Austria and issues an ultimatum that he relent upon threat of armed invasion. When Schuschnigg capitulates, Hitler demands that he resign. Schuschnigg does so on March 11, after which Austria becomes part of Germany.

Encouraged by events in Austria, Czechoslovakian National Socialists demand cession of the Sudetenland (a predominantly German-speaking area of country) to Germany, which demand is rejected by the Czech government. Hitler mobilizes troops along the Czechoslovakian border; the Czechs do likewise. When Hitler reveals his intent to invade Czechoslovakia, Beck resigns. Czech Nazis foment widespread disorder, causing the government to declare martial law. At a September 15 meeting with Britain Prime Minister Neville Chamberlain, Hitler states that Germany will invade unless the Czech government permits Sudetenland residents to vote on whether to secede from the country. When Chamberlain counsels the Czechs to assent to Hitler's demands, Russia declares that it will defend the Czechs if France will do the same. Not satisfied with Czech Premier Milan Hodza's assent to his demand for a referendum, Hitler threatens invasion if German occupation of Sudetenland is not granted by October 1, which demand is rejected by the Czechs. Chamberlain, Hitler, France's Edouard Daladier, and Italy's Benito Mussolini conclude the Munich Pact on September 29, giving in to all of Hitler's demands despite the absence of Czech and Russian representation. Britain's Chamberlain claims to have achieved "peace in our time".

With Finkenwalde closed by the Gestapo, the Confessing Church begins operating underground seminaries, assigning students to parishes in obscure areas, while actually gathering them for classes. Dietrich teaches at two such seminaries in eastern Pomerania, escaping observation by registering as the curate of parish in Schlawe. Here he writes *Life Together*, a study of what it means to be a Christian community. He also works to boost the morale of Finkenwalde graduates, who are being denied positions unless pledging loyalty to Hitler. While in Pomerania, Dietrich frequents the estate of Frau Ruth von Kleist-Retzow, a Confessing Church financial supporter, where he meets Ewald von Kleist and Fabian von Schlabrendorff, and first encounters discussion of Resistance.

Dietrich begins to make frequent trips to Berlin, entry into which was forbidden him by the Gestapo if on church business, taking part in meetings at his parents' home on Marienburger-Alle where discussions of Resistance are being held. His sister, Ursula, and husband Rudiger Schleicher live next door. Sister Christine and husband Hans von Dohnanyi live nearby. Hans, Assistant to the Minister of Justice, is in a losing battle to keep Germany's legal system free from Nazi influence. He is also assembling a *Chronicle of Scandals*, secretly documenting all of the political injustices committed by the Reich. His research brings him in contact with Admiral Wilhelm Canaris, head of Counter-Intelligence, Major General Hans Oster, second in command at Counter-Intelligence, and Dr. Karl Sack, Judge Advocate General. Privy to inside information, Hans informs the Marienburger-Alle group of Hitler's preparations for war months before they are made public.

Hans and Dietrich are close friends, Hans often turning to Dietrich for guidance. One evening he asks, "in what sense should one understand the New Testament passage in which Jesus warns his disciples that they who take the sword shall perish by the sword". Dietrich replies that the passage must be taken at face value and that it is valid for all times. Christians must accept the fact that they too come under the power of that judgment, but that the times have need of men who are willing to take it upon themselves.

Tipped by Hans that increased oppression of the Jewish people is likely once Hitler initiates hostilities, Dietrich and Bethge help his twin, Sabine, her husband Gerhard Leibholz, and their young daughters flee to Switzerland and from there to Oxford, England. Feigning a holiday to Basel, the family escapes after a tearful farewell and a drive through the night.

A critical moment for Dietrich occurs during a lecture on Romans 13, "let every soul be subject to the higher powers." Challenged by Helmuth Traub regarding the role of resistance in light of Romans 13, Dietrich responds privately that while a Christian must not act impulsively or irresponsibly he must be willing to abandon "the protective enclosure of Churchliness", but not the Church, if his witness is to have any value. Dietrich realizes that the only way to avert war is to overthrow the Nazi government.

The Resistance fails in its first attempt to stop Hitler. The plan calls for complicit officers to seize Hitler the moment he gives the command to invade Czechoslovakia and to bring him before a People's Court, where Hans and Sack will prosecute him for irresponsibly involving the country in war, with expert witness given by Dietrich's father and his fellow psychiatrists. Once Hitler is declared unfit for office, a military government will convene until elections can be held, with General Beck being given the reigns of power during the interim. Kleist and other distinguished emissaries are sent to Britain to inform them of plans for the coup. Nevertheless, although aware of the imminent coup, Chamberlain flies to Munich on the very eve of the attempt, signs the Munich Pact, and spoils everything.

On November 7, a crazed Jewish teenager assassinates a German military officer in Paris, after which the Nazis embark upon a night of terror, destroying Jewish synagogues, shops, and houses throughout the Reich. When hardly a peep is heard from the Confessing Church regarding this "Night of Broken Glass", Dietrich concludes that Confessing Church efforts have failed. And when his age group is about to be called into military service, Dietrich, who realizes he could never fight to maintain a Nazi state, makes a short visit to Bishop Bell in England and to Willem Visser 'tHooft,

Secretary of the newly-formed World Council of Churches in Switzerland, to inquire about the possibility of making a lecture tour in America.

1939

After having been granted the Sudetenland by the Munich Pact, Hitler proceeds to simply take the rest of Czechoslovakia, acquiring vast stores of military and industrial advantages that will aide him in World War II. Having successfully bullied his way to get what he wanted in Czechoslovakia, he next demands that Poland cede the Polish Corridor and the free city of Danzig, citing the Soviet communist threat as reason both for this and his takeover of Czechoslovakia. Poland rejects his demands.

American theologians Reinhold Niebuhr and Paul Lehmann arrange lecture tour of the USA for Dietrich. Henry Leiper of the Council of Churches secures a summer appointment for him at Union Theological Seminary, and a more permanent position as pastor to German refugees in New York, the latter of which Dietrich is unaware. Leaving for New York on June 4 with his brother, Karl-Friedrich, who also has a lecture tour, Dietrich struggles daily with his decision. Upon learning of the refugee appointment, Dietrich realizes that his acceptance will preclude his return to Germany, and thus declines. After an evening's solitary walk in the Times Square, deep in thought, Dietrich concludes that it was wrong for him to have left the struggle in Germany, and that he must return. Leiper doesn't understand and is disappointed in him, causing Dietrich to write Bethge, "It is strange, in any decision, I am never quite clear about my motives. Is that a sign of uncertainty, inner dishonesty, or is it a sign that God leads us over and beyond our own powers of discernment." Lehmann arrives in New York and fails to dissuade Dietrich, who boards ship and sails from New York at midnight on July 7.

Dietrich returns to teach at the underground seminaries in the Pomeranian Forest. He begins writing his *Ethics*, which emanates not from some ivory tower, but, as biographer, Mary Bosanquet, put it, "from the cauldron of agonizing decisions that could mean life or death for the body and salvation or damnation for the soul".

After having signed a non-aggression pact with the USSR just one week prior, Hitler invades Poland from the West on September 1 while the USSR rushes in from the East, causing France and Britain to declare war on Germany September 3. In an utter display of barbarity, storm troopers systematically exterminate Polish citizens on order of the Nazi Party, much to the disgust of the regular German soldier. The two aggressors, Germany and USSR, establish a line of demarcation in Poland. The surviving Poles are herded off to concentration camps.

The Resistance increases its efforts. The Beck group favors a democratic state following the overthrow of the Nazis. A separate Resistance group, the "Kreisau Circle," lays plans for a Socialist Utopia. Both realize that Germany will eventually be defeated. Ulrich von Hassell serves as liaison between the two Resistance groups. Of critical importance is gaining assurance from Britain that it will negotiate with the Resistance after the war. The initial approach to discuss this with Britain is made through the Vatican by Joseph Muller, a Catholic attorney, and documented in Hans' secret files. When two British spies are captured along the border with Holland, and an ex-communist (unassociated with the Resistance) attempts to assassinate Hitler, German newspapers at the direction of Goebbels craftily connect the two events, blame the assassination attempt on Britain, whip up popular sentiment for the war, and renders the success of the Resistance's request of Britain less likely.

1940

The underground seminaries in Pomerania are discovered by the Gestapo in January and shut down. Dietrich maintains contact with Finkenwalde graduates, endeavoring to encourage them, while having to report the increasing number of their fellows who are being killed on the front.

The Soviets conquer Finland in March. Germany conquers Norway, Belgium, Holland, and Luxembourg in May. Winston Churchill replaces Chamberlain as British Prime Minister and the evacuation of Dunkirk begins May 27. Germany captures Paris June 14. The Soviets annex Lithuania, Estonia, and Latvia in June, and begin to mobilize for taking the Balkans. Hitler, wanting the Balkans for himself, must decide whether to fight the Soviets, and thus battle on two fronts.

Dietrich's conference with students in July is broken up by the Gestapo, saying that even such meetings are now outlawed. Dietrich heads to Berlin and, after conferring with Hans, Oster, and Canaris, signs on at Counter-Intelligence, thus preventing his conscription into the military and protecting him from the Gestapo. The latter nonetheless cites Dietrich for "subversive activity", forbids him to speak in public, and requires him to report regularly from his "official place of residence". Counter-Intelligence accordingly reassigns Dietrich to its Munich office, far from Berlin, where he takes up "official residence". Living in the Ettal Hotel and eating in the Abbey (whose monks are likewise involved in the Resistance), Dietrich spends the winter months in the library working on his *Ethics*.

Hitler attacks Britain daily with 1,000 German bombers, a prelude to invasion. Churchill rallies a few hundred Royal Air Force pilots in small fighter craft and begins to beat back the onslaught, turning the tide. On August 21, the RAF destroys 200 German planes, a feat it repeats daily. The RAF eventually reaches Germany and begins to destroy its war-supply factories. Germany switches tactics and begins to concentrate 500 planes per day on one specific target, changing that target daily. London endures a horrid bombing on December 29, after which RAF bombing of German factories begins to pay off. German air attacks lessen, and within weeks Germany acknowledges that it cannot defeat the RAF and abandons its invasion plans.

1941

Dietrich travels to Switzerland, ostensibly as a Counter-Intelligence agent, to implore Visser 'tHooft to contact Bishop Bell to discover whether the British government would be willing to negotiate peace with the Resistance. When Visser 'tHooft asks, "For what do you pray in these days?" Dietrich replies, "If you want to know the truth, I pray for the defeat of my nation, for I believe that is the only way to pay for all the suffering which my country has caused in the world." While in Switzerland, Dietrich meets with Barth, who cannot fathom his involvement in counter-espionage, which includes members of the Gestapo, government officials, Secret Service agents, and a complex web of deception. The Gestapo eventually rescinds its demand that Dietrich report to them, after which he moves back to Berlin. However, the Gestapo now forbids him to publish.

After subjugating Yugoslavia and Greece in April, Hitler invades the USSR on June 22, leading Churchill to forge a mutual-aid pact with the Soviets. The USA begins lending non-military aid to Great Britain.

When Churchill rejects cooperating with the Resistance, Dietrich makes a second trip to Geneva to encourage a renewed effort to convince the British. Upon his return to Germany, he becomes involved in U7, the attempt to smuggle Jewish people across the border into Switzerland.

Japan attacks Pearl Harbor December 7. The USA declares war on Japan the following day, after which Germany and Italy declare war on the US. Hitler assumes tactical command of the German war machine, a major blunder. The Resistance swings into high gear. Dietrich states that he would be willing to take part in an attempt on Hitler's life if this were required of him, fully realizing that this would doom his career as a pastor.

1942

Dietrich and Hans discover that the Gestapo is censoring their mail and tapping their telephones. They persevere.

Subsequent to the Nazi takeover in Norway, the Provost of Trodheim Cathedral is dismissed, which causes Norway pastors to refuse to perform their duties. Thousands of schoolteachers resign when it is announced that a "Hitler Youth" program is to be established in the country. As a consequence, the leader of the Norwegian Resistance, Elvind Berggrav, is imprisoned. To end the crisis, German Counter-Intelligence (secretly led by members of the Resistance) argues that these actions by the Norwegian government only encourage the people to obstruct the German war effort. It therefore presses for the release of Berggrav and sends Dietrich to Norway, ostensibly to implement general pacification, but actually to strengthen the Resistance there.

On his third trip to Switzerland, Dietrich finds no one with whom he can speak. However, he learns that Bishop Bell is in Sweden, which presents Dietrich with an opportunity for direct contact. He rushes to Berlin and obtains permission to travel to Sweden on behalf of Counter-Intelligence. Upon his arrival, Dietrich finds Bell being visited by Hans Schoenfeld, the Reich Church Foreign representative in Geneva, whose cooperation with the Resistance was considered by Dietrich to be suspect. A nervous Schoenfeld spills detailed information about the German Resistance and asks whether Britain would consider negotiating peace with a new government. Bell is suspicious of Schoenfeld due to the latter's ties to the Reich Church. In a tactical error, Dietrich confirms what Schoenfeld has said, even supplying the names of those involved in the conspiracy. Bell returns to England, resolved to do all he can to sway Britain's attitude toward a reconstituted German government. However, he finds that the British are past wanting to hear of German Resistance and think only in terms of unconditional surrender. Bell continues to speak on behalf of the Resistance in the House of Lords in the face of impassioned opposition and at the risk of his own reputation. His pleas go unheeded.

Dietrich returns to Pomerania and is introduced to Kleist-Retzow's granddaughter, Maria von Wedemeyer. When Maria's father is subsequently killed on Russian front, Dietrich writes her mother a consoling letter, and begins to visit Maria on a frequent basis, both in Pomerania and in Berlin (where she is a nursing student). Dietrich's hope for the future increases.

The Gestapo is hot on the trail of Counter-Intelligence (its archrival) and connects it with U7. It also questions Dietrich's involvement and his corresponding deferment from conscription into the armed forces. Aware that the Gestapo is hot on their trail, the Resistance makes detailed plans for cover-up in case of capture. Notes to misdirect investigators are imbedded into Counter-Intelligence files, and Hans travels to Switzerland to brief U7 beneficiaries what to say should they be interrogated

Maria prevails upon her mother, who two months prior had imposed a yearlong separation between Maria and Dietrich due to their 17-year age difference and Dietrich's involvement in dangerous activities. Dietrich and Maria become engaged.

The Soviets, with arms aid from the USA, rebuff Hitler at Stalingrad, a major turning point in the war. The Resistance makes a second attempt on Hitler's life March 13. Following lunch with Hitler's entourage, General Henning von Tresckow requests that General Heinz Brandt take two bottles of brandy to General Helmuth Stieff in Rastenberg. Brandt agrees and Schlabrendorff gives Brandt a package containing the bomb-laden bottles as the latter accompanies Hitler's entourage onto the plane. The bomb's fuse is for 30 minutes into the two-hour flight. Tresckow and Schlabrendorff, listening intently to the military radio, are dumbfounded to learn that Hitler's plane lands in Rastenburg without incident. In a panic, Tresckow telephones Brandt, states that a mix-up has occurred, and promises to have Schlabrendorff there the next day to give him the correct package. After a nervous flight, Schlabrendorff is able to switch packages and dismantle the bomb.

One week later, a third attempt is made. Major Rudolf von Gersdorff plants plastic bombs in each of his coat pockets, sets a five-minute fuse, and ventures into the crowded Berlin Armory, where Hitler is observing an exhibit of captured war materials. His plan to embrace Hitler and sacrifice his own life in order to end Hitler's is thwarted when the dictator suddenly leaves the exhibition. Gersdorff hurries into a public restroom just in time to dismantle the bombs. Dietrich, Hans, brother Klaus, and brother-in-law Rudiger, each privy to the plot, wait in vain at Marienburger-Alle for a telephone call regarding the success of the attempt, while they and their families rehearse a cantata to be performed at father Karl's upcoming 75th birthday party.

On April 5, Dietrich's phone call to the home of Hans and Christine is answered gruffly by an unfamiliar voice. Dietrich realizes that Hans and Christine are being arrested and that the Gestapo will be at Marienburger-Alle next. So not to worry his parents, he goes next door and asks sister Ursula to prepare him a large meal, knowing it may be his last for some time. Returning home, Dietrich makes a last check for incriminating papers, leaves misguiding notes, and then returns to the Schleicher's to wait with them and Bethge. After a while, his father looks in and says, "Dietrich, two men want to see you in your room." Gestapo Chief Investigator Manfred Roeder and Franz Sonderegger order Dietrich to accompany them to their car. The black

Mercedes drives away quietly, taking Dietrich to the Tegel Military Prison in Berlin. Christine is later released.

During the cold night, Dietrich doesn't use the foul smelling blanket provided him, nor does he get much sleep due to the continual sobbing of a prisoner in next cell. In the morning, a piece of bread is thrown onto the floor through the observation hole. Upon learning that Dietrich is a pastor, the guards and prisoners begin to seek him out, after which he is shackled and put into solitary confinement with a note prohibiting access to him without permission. No one speaks to Dietrich for the next 12 days; it is just food thrown in and waste taken out. He writes, "At first I wondered a great deal whether it was really for the cause of Christ that I was causing you all such grief."

Cover-up plans call for Hans to take full responsibility for questionable activities at Counter-Intelligence and for Canaris, still at liberty, to confirm that all activities were done with his approval and in the interests of the Counter-Intelligence effort. The Resistance sends messages to Hans and Dietrich by means of books in which the owner's name is underlined on the flyleaf, and beginning from the end of the book, letters are marked very faintly.

As Allied air raids increase, Dietrich's knowledge of first aid is utilized in the prison clinic, where he converses with prisoner and guard alike. Maria is granted visiting rights, which proves very painful. Dietrich later writes, "I often wonder who I really am—the man who goes on squirming under these ghastly experiences in wretchedness that cries to heaven, or the man who scourges himself and pretends to others (and even to himself) that he is placid, cheerful, composed, and in control of himself, and allows people to admire him for it."

With Hans about to break after seven months of intense interrogation, an Allied bomb explodes in his Lehrterstrasse cell, leaving him partially paralyzed with cerebral thrombosis. He is sent to the Prison Hospital in Buchenwald.

1944

A fourth attempt on Hitler's life was to be made by Stieff, whom Hitler called a "poisonous little dwarf", but the explosives stored under a tower detonate prematurely and unexpectedly. Yet another attempt was to be by Captain Axel von Bussche, using bombs concealed in the pockets of a new military uniform he was to model for Hitler. However, Allied bombing destroyed the factory making the uniforms. Attempt six was to be Kleist, also modeling a uniform, but an air raid just prior cancelled the event. Attempt seven was to feature Captain Eberhard von Brietenbuch smuggling a concealed pistol into Hitler's Berghof Villa, but he is denied proximity to Hitler due to his lower rank.

In April, Sack counsels rather than to hope for quick release via trial and acquittal, imprisoned Resistance members should "vanish into the sand", allowing one's case to fall into the background in the hope that Germany will soon be defeated. Accordingly, Dietrich puts all thought of release out of mind and begins a theological correspondence with Bethge, which is posthumously published as *Letters and Papers from Prison*. Surrounded by prisoners for whom religion is irrelevant and meaningless, Dietrich argues for a religionless Christianity: the removal of man-made trappings that have made Christianity just one more religion. He calls for focus on Christ alone.

The Allies invade Normandy on June 6, the second critical turning point in the war. A final attempt on Hitler's life takes place July 20 as Stauffenberg, now with direct access to Hitler, manages to set a bomb-laden briefcase next to Hitler under a table over which he and his generals are examining maps and plotting war strategy at the Wolf's Lair in Rastenburg. The briefcase, however, is absentmindedly removed to the far end of the table by one of the attendees whose foot had accidentally hit it. Stauffenberg escapes the room under pretense just prior to a massive explosion from which Hitler escapes with only minor cuts and bruises. Stauffenberg is captured and shot later that day, Beck commits suicide, and Canaris and Oster are arrested. Hitler uses the event as an excuse to round up all of whom he is suspicious. The Resistance has failed.

Dietrich realizes his chances of escape are remote, writing on July 21, "I am still discovering, right up to this moment, that it is only by living completely in this world that one learns to have faith. One must completely abandon any attempt to make something of oneself ... and live unreservedly in life's duties, problems, successes and failures, experiences and perplexities. In so doing, we throw ourselves completely into the arms of God, taking seriously, not our own sufferings, but those of God in the world... That, I think, is faith... and that is how one becomes a man and a Christian."

On September 20, while plodding through material removed from the Counter-Intelligence office, Sonderegger discovers a secret file containing documents that incriminate members of the Resistance beyond dispute: plans for a coup in Oster's handwriting, a record of discussions with Britain through the Vatican, excerpts from Canaris' diary about recruiting members for the Resistance, details of Dietrich's activities, etc.

An attempt to free Dietrich is set in motion September 24 as Ursula and Rudiger, together with Bethge and his wife, Renate, meet a trusted prison guard on the outskirts of Berlin, give him food, a ration card, and clothes to hide in a shed for latter use by Dietrich and himself once the Tegel guard has helped Dietrich escape. However, upon learning that brother Klaus and brother-in-law Rudiger have been arrested, Dietrich sends a note to Marienburger-Alle stating that he has given up the plan to escape for fear of reprisals against Klaus, Rudiger, Hans, and the family. On October 8, Dietrich is transferred to Berlin's Prinz Albrecht Strasse prison, which already houses Schlabrendorff, Oster, Canaris, and Joseph Muller. Hans is taken to Sachsenhausen. Hitler orders that executions of the conspirators be delayed until he can elicit the names of other Resistance members by means of torture.

1945

The Battle of the Bulge, Germany's final thrust in the West, is offset by a major Soviet attack in the East. Allied bombing paralyzes Berlin. Meeting at Yalta, Roosevelt, Churchill, and Stalin lay plans for post-war Europe following unconditional German surrender. Germany refuses to give up.

Hans sneaks a note to Christine in minute letters written on a tin can lid. His request: that diphtheria be blended into a specially marked food container and sent to him. Hans hopes that his resulting sickness will preclude future torture and his unwitting revelation of fellow conspirators. Hans is shortly in the hospital once again. Christine returns from a futile attempt to deliver birthday greetings to Dietrich, unaware that he has been taken to Buchenwald. Canaris, Oster, and Sack are taken to Flossenburg, an extermination camp. Bell writes to Gerhard concerning Dietrich, "May God spare him for the survival of the Church in Germany and the world."

Germany is in chaos, crushed by Allied advances from East and West. Maria sets out alone in the bitter cold to search for Dietrich. She is unsuccessful. At Buchenwald, Payne Best, one of the British spies captured along the border with Holland, observes of Dietrich, "He was different than the others; quite calm and normal, seemingly perfectly at ease ... his soul really shone in the dark desperation of our prison ... all humility and sweetness ... always seemed to diffuse an atmosphere of happiness, of joy in every smallest event in life, and of deep gratitude for the mere fact that he was alive. He was one of the very few men I have ever met to whom his God was real, and ever close to him." With the Nazi war machine disintegrating, the Allies race across Germany, meeting little opposition.

On April 1, Easter Sunday, the prisoners take hope at the sound of Allied guns in the distance. Hitler orders that all who were involved in the conspiracy be executed. Dietrich and his fellow prisoners are squeezed into the back of a wood-burning prison van (petrol is scarce), which chugs away at 20 miles per hour, stopping every 15 minutes to have its cylinders cleaned and for enough steam to be generated by the fire for operating the engine. With no food, they travel day and night toward Flossenburg, reaching Weiden on April 4, 12 miles at the foot of the valley that hides the extermination camp. They are told to continue driving south; the camp is too full. Soon overtaken by motorized police, Dietrich leans back into the shadows as three prisoners are called out. The wood-burning truck heads further south. On April 5, the truck skids to halt with broken steering. On April 6, the prisoners are transferred into a comfortable bus. Sprits rise. They meander along the Danube River, rising into the Bavarian forest, reaching the small town of Schonberg, high in the mountains. The prisoners are locked into a schoolhouse with beds, linens, covers, and curtained windows. Kind-hearted villagers bring them a loaf of bread and a bowl of potatoes.

On April 6, Gestapo Judge Walter Huppenkothen arrives in Sachsenhausen, sentences Hans to death, and then heads for Flossenburg. Dietrich is missing. Schlabrendorff is awakened twice in the middle of the night and accused of being Dietrich.

On Sunday, April 8, the hopeful prisoners ask Dietrich to hold a worship service. He consents and talks about Isaiah 53, "with his stripes we are healed," and 1 Peter 1:3 regarding our "lively hope by the resurrection of Jesus Christ from the dead." Suddenly, the door flings open. The guard shouts, "Prisoner Bonhoeffer, come with us." Dietrich says to Payne Best, "This is the end, but for me the beginning of life." Dietrich bounds down the stairs and into the waiting prison van. In the dead of night, the conspirators in Flossenburg are confronted with each other and condemned to death. Between five and six o'clock on the morning of April 9, the guard finds Dietrich kneeling in his cell, praying. He is ordered to strip, is led to the execution site together with Canaris, Oster, Sack and the others, and is hung. Hans, Klaus, and Rudiger are shot to death.

Hitler kills himself April 30. Berlin falls May 2. Germany surrenders May 7. Dietrich's parents, unaware of his fate, come across a Memorial Service being broadcast on the BBC July 27, hearing Franz Hildebrandt eulogize, "In his capacity to return from agonizing questions to the cheerful discipleship of Jesus Christ lies the secret of Dietrich Bonhoeffer."

Bibliography

Bethge, Eberhard, *Dietrich Bonhoeffer: A Biography*, Fortress Press, 2000.

Bosanquet, Mary, *The Life and Death of Dietrich Bonhoeffer*, Harper & Row, 1968.

Shirer, William L., *The Rise and Fall of the Third Reich: A History of Nazi Germany*, Fawcett Crest, 1950, 1960.

About the Author

In addition to *Bonhoeffer: A Screenplay*, William Wilson has written three other books, *God & You: Restoring the Relationship*, *New America: A National Renaissance*, and *95 Theses for Skeptic, Church, and Nation*, has been a guest columnist for several newspapers, and has worked in the fields of education and social services. He has received degrees from Concordia University Nebraska, Concordia Seminary, and the College of William & Mary, and writes from his home in Johnston, Iowa, where he lives with his wife, Lynn.

Made in the USA
Lexington, KY
22 January 2019